MARTHA'S VINEYARD

in

WORLD WAR II

MARTHA'S VINEYARD

in

WORLD WAR II

Thomas Dresser

THOMAS DRESSER, HERB FOSTER
& JAY SCHOFIELD

October 17, 2019

THE
History
PRESS

Published by The History Press
Charleston, SC 29403
www.historypress.net

First published 2014
Second printing 2014

Manufactured in the United States

ISBN 978.1.62619.372.7

Library of Congress Cataloging-in-Publication Data

Dresser, Tom.
Martha's Vineyard in World War II / Thomas Dresser, Herb Foster and Jay Schofield.
pages cm
Includes bibliographical references and index.
ISBN 978-1-62619-372-7
1. World War, 1939-1945--Massachusetts--Martha's Vineyard. 2. Martha's Vineyard
(Mass.)--History--20th century. I. Foster, Herbert L. II. Schofield, Jay, 1942- III. Title.
D769.85.M41M374 2014
940.53'74494--dc23
2014010152

This book is dedicated to the servicemen and women and citizens of Martha's Vineyard who gave so much during World War II.

CONTENTS

CONTENTS

FOREWORD

During World War II, the entire Vineyard community mobilized to support the war effort, both on the homefront and overseas. Vineyard men and women served abroad in every theater of the war. The Vineyard's location made it a strategic outpost for both military training and coastal communications and surveillance.

In the early 1940s, the island became a bustling center of military activity. One square mile of land at the heart of the state forest was taken by the federal government to construct the Martha's Vineyard Naval Auxiliary Air Facility (now the Martha's Vineyard Airport) for training new pilots and for "R&R" and refresher courses for seasoned airmen. The military maintained installations at the Vineyard's high ground on Peaked Hill in Chilmark and at a gunnery training facility in Katama. Ground and air training maneuvers were carried out along the island's north and south shore beaches, with landing forces often making incursions into the island's interior and wooded areas. New roads were built. The United States Coast Guard was on high alert in Gay Head, Chappaquiddick and every corner of the island. Civilian Defense and United Service Organizations (USOs) were active in island towns. The lives of Vineyarders of all ages were affected by the wartime activity, and islanders responded with shared sacrifice and embraced civil defense responsibilities through a range of civilian support activities.

In my work conducting oral history interviews on Martha's Vineyard for more than twenty-five years, the stories and recollections of World

War II are among the most poignant and powerful. The personal stories and perspectives of Vineyard people who lived through the war years bring alive in a powerful way the tenor and emotions of that difficult time.

Hearing stories in the words of neighbors you know can bring a distant time and experience to life. We can feel and relate much more closely to the stories from those who served overseas of their longing for their island home and family and the horror and confusion of battle. Hearing the words of those who stayed on the island, we get a sense of how acutely Vineyarders of all ages were affected by the war. In the stories from servicemen assigned to this island outpost (for many of them, a place of which they had never heard), we see how the Vineyard and its people had a profound, often lifelong impact on these young soldiers and airmen, fostering bonds of friendship and marriage.

Events from those times that register in memory are deeply personal and subjective: thoughts of peace while sitting in a shack heated by a potbelly stove by the East Chop Lighthouse watching for enemy planes; nervousness while patrolling the pitch-dark streets of Vineyard Haven, checking for lights-out; applying makeup to one's legs to mimic nylon stockings; adding vials of orange food coloring to make unpleasant-tasting rationed margarine resemble butter; wrapping gum wrappers and tin foil into balls for the war effort; the excitement and fear of rumors of submarines off Gay Head and Squibnocket.

These are the details and feelings that make the past uniquely accessible to us. And these stories will open your eyes and help you see the island in a different way. The wooden building you pass on Beach Road housed a workshop where talented island craftsmen built ship and airplane silhouettes and models for combat training. The Cronig's Real Estate building on Main Street in Vineyard Haven was the hub for USO activity on the island, welcoming servicemen from Peaked Hill and the Naval Air facilities. Through these stories, we become so aware that the past is always around us.

It is vital to collect and preserve these personal recollections to further our understanding of a past that we can use to help shape a better future. Also, we must never forget the tragedies and triumphs, the momentous moments and small happenings that have made us who we are. These stories and photos assembled and skillfully interwoven here by Tom Dresser, Jay Schofield and Herb Foster bring alive to us a pivotal time in the history of the people of the Vineyard. Looking through these Vineyard-colored lenses helps us understand a vital time in world history.

The personal and emotional dimension provided by oral histories transports the reader and enlivens the past in a unique way. While we share in the joys and sorrows of these individuals, we are also reminded of the tremendous importance of their sacrifice during this critical period in the history of the twentieth century.

The vitality of these recollections and the preservation of the photographs, diaries and letters through the years, in closets, basements and photo albums, indicates the impact the war had on the lives of the men and women of the Vineyard community.

Linsey Lee
Curator of Oral History
Martha's Vineyard Museum

For more than twenty-five years, Linsey Lee has collected oral histories on Martha's Vineyard. She is the author of *Vineyard Voices: Words, Faces and Voices of Island People*, 1998; *More Vineyard Voices*, 2006; *Those Who Serve: Martha's Vineyard and World War II*, 2011; and *Edible Wild Plants of Martha's Vineyard*, 1976.

———◆———

To listen to audio tapes edited from World War II oral histories, visit the Martha's Vineyard Museum: www.mvmuseum.org/wwii.php.

THE INVASION
OF MARTHA'S VINEYARD

Wednesday, August 19, 1942. "The war is on. Awakened at 5 am by the roaring of motor boats and planes and shots in the direction of Seven Gates, sounding like the 4th of July. Out of bed before six and after attending to the oil difficulties, and orange juice and coffee, put on my hip rubber boots and went up on the hill. Nothing to be seen but hundreds of boats in the Sound and planes overhead."[1]

Seventy-four-year-old retired newspaper editor George A. Hough (1868–1955) was jolted awake at that early morning hour by armed forces invading the bucolic island of Martha's Vineyard. Hough was a responsible reporter; he maintained journals of his Vineyard experiences from 1899 until his death. He lived at Fish Hook on Indian Hill, in West Tisbury, and also owned the nearby Ephriam Allen house. Retired as editor of the *New Bedford Evening Standard*, Hough was father to George Hough, editor of the *Falmouth Enterprise*, and Henry Beetle Hough, editor of the *Vineyard Gazette*; he was the great-grandfather of author John Hough.

The invading force, as Hough was well aware, was made up of GIs from the Forty-fifth Infantry Division in a United States Army training maneuver, staging a practice attack to re-capture Martha's Vineyard from the "Germans."

Just days before the mock invasion, on August 14, Hough had recorded in his diary, "Fish Hook swarming with many officers at noon in two jeeps—colonels, lieutenants, captains. Visited Allen house with which they seemed [satisfied] for staff H.Q." Hough was proud of his involvement.

"Served scotch on Fish Hook porch to head of defending commander of Martha's Vineyard and others." That evening, they sat by the radio, listening to an interview with the commander of the WAVES (Women Accepted for Voluntary Emergency Service).

———————

Earlier in that summer of 1942, Henry Beetle Hough had been notified of the impending invasion by the army and published a notice in his *Vineyard Gazette*: "Large scale maneuvers are to be undertaken here, and the Army is announcing the plan in order to obtain the cooperation of the public."

Field exercises would entail ferrying troops from Camp Edwards, on Cape Cod, across Vineyard Sound, with "landing operations along the north shore in the region lying generally between Chappaquonsett and Cape Higgon."[2] (This spanned from Vineyard Haven to Chilmark.)

Plans called for a defending force on the Vineyard, consisting of local state guard companies. While the army sought permission from local landowners for the invasion, it promised not to destroy private property. The *Gazette* opined, "There is no doubt that the necessity for giving war training a right of way will be understood on the Vineyard."

The word "jeep" is an abbreviated form of the initials GP, for general purpose vehicle. This army jeep, with trailer, is owned by Gary Soares, a U.S. Marine Corps veteran and collector/ historian. "I collect militaria from all wars, Revolutionary to Afghanistan." It makes him feel close to history. *Property of Gary Soares, on display at Camp Edwards; photo by Joyce Dresser.*

A soldier (reenactor Steve Abatemarco) with contents of the forty-eight-pound pack borne by World War II soldiers. *Photo by Joyce Dresser.*

The *Gazette* urged landowners to "be good sports. They should not be excited or angry." Trespassers' rights had been requested and granted for permission to train soldiers. The army wanted rights on "every available foot" of Vineyard soil and ominously noted that even without permission, training would proceed on schedule. If property was damaged, however, the owner was to write Camp Edwards explaining the circumstances, and the matter should be resolved.

The Forbes family granted permission for the army to use their Elizabeth islands of Naushon, Nashawena and Pasque for military maneuvers. Editor Hough noted that Jimmy Cagney had offered his Chilmark home on North Road to staff officers for impending army activities. And another Vineyarder, John Daggett, wrote, "A group of top officers took quarters in our house for a week for various conferences and the making of plans for the training of the men preparatory to the invasion of the Continent. These preparations for war were exciting, but they had a grim side too."[3]

The *Gazette* added the comforting comments that the invasion would not occur for a few weeks and live ammunition would not be used.

John Daggett told of the role his homestead played: "Our beach, as well as many other places on the north side of the Island, was frequently visited by dozens of small LCI (landing craft, infantry) boats carrying large numbers of men who embarked from the general vicinity of Cotuit on Cape Cod."[4]

Riley Deeble, of West Tisbury, recalled, "Retired Major General Preston Brown had built his house across from the entrance to Lambert's Cove Beach. It's a big house, with a large lawn, right on the curve [still extant]. He saw this thing coming, and he took the precaution of going to a print shop and getting signs that said, 'Off limits.' Soldiers would not tramp on his property." Not everyone was eager to have army men stomping on their green grass and flowers.

ACKNOWLEDGEMENTS

Herb came up with the idea of writing a book about Martha's Vineyard during World War II. Jay has written several books about the war, as well as Vineyard biographies. And Tom loves anything about Vineyard history. That's how the book came together. Herb cruised the Internet to find fascinating sites to buttress our research. Jay interviewed people for their life stories and supplemented earlier Vineyard interviews with current islander interviews. Tom haunted the microfiche files of the *Vineyard Gazette*, focusing on the war years. Herb developed the story of Peaked Hill. Jay worked on the airfield. Tom covered the invasion. We added to one another's work. And like a trio of romeos (retired old men eating out), we met each week at Woodland Variety & Grill in Vineyard Haven for a bite to eat and to share our latest "nuggets."

We recognize the many people whom we interviewed. Their patience for our literary effort is greatly appreciated. Several individuals deserve to be singled out: John Alley, Megan Alley, Hector Asselin, Chris Baer, Jackie Baer, Ann Barry, Don Bender, Donald Billings, Carol Carr, Timothy Carroll, Dave Chickering, Richard Clark, Cynthia Cowan, Riley Deeble, Tom Dunlop, Francis Fisher, Connie Frank, John Galluzzo, John Hough, Leonard Jason, Chris Kennedy, Dave Larsen, Linsey Lee, David Maciel, Bud Mayhew, Donald Mayhew, Joe McLaughlin, Ian Meisner, Larry Mercier, JoAnn Murphy, Nancy Nitchie, Herman Page, Tom Page, Pete Payette, Everett Poole, Rosalie Powell, Tag Rainsford, Jane Slater, Russ Smith, Ruth Stiller, Bob Tankard, Susan Thompson, Bob Tilton, Bow Van Ryper and Terre Young.

Martha's Vineyard is nearly one hundred square miles in area; east to west is approximately twenty miles, and north to south is ten miles. *Map drawn by Joyce Dresser.*

Books proved invaluable to our research, especially three by Linsey Lee of the Martha's Vineyard Museum: *Vineyard Voices*, *More Vineyard Voices* and *Those Who Serve*. Each book captures essential elements of people who lived on Martha's Vineyard; the interviews dramatically supplemented our research.

Organizations that provided assistance include Camp Edwards; Mark Berhow of the Coast Defense Study Group; Edgartown Public Library; Falmouth Historical Society; Adrienne Latimer of the Falmouth Library; Bob Clark of the Franklin D. Roosevelt Presidential Library & Museum; Thomas Weiss of the Library of Contemporary History, Stuttgart, Germany; Erin Lopater of Mariners' Museum and Park; Nathaniel Janick of the Martha's Vineyard Museum; MVTV; Libby Oldham of the Nantucket Historical Society; National Archives (in Waltham and College Park, Maryland); Anna Marie D'Addarie of Oak Bluffs Library; Quonset Air Museum; the U.S.

Army Corps of Engineers; Hilary Wall of the *Vineyard Gazette*; Betty Burton of Vineyard Haven Library; Carol Magee of VOLF (Vineyard Open Land Foundation); Duane Watson of the Wilderstein Historic Site; and Susan Witzell of the Woods Hole Historical Museum.

And this book would not have become reality without the patience and support of History Press commissioning editor Tabitha Dulla, marketing expertise of Katie Parry, copyediting by Hilary Parrish and a dynamic sales manager with Dani McGrath. Tom's wife, Joyce, read through the manuscript thrice with a careful pen, took photos for the illustrations and drew the map of the Vineyard. Thanks for your support and encouragement along the way.

There you have it. We spent months researching, interviewing, writing and editing. Now it's time to publish. It's been a great ride!

TOURING MARTHA'S VINEYARD IN THE 1930s[5]

Before the war, travel to Martha's Vineyard was an adventure. In the 1930s, you had to go to New Bedford, where the New England Steamship Company provided ferry service. The trip to the Vineyard cost one dollar and took two hours. If you could afford a car, the cost for its transport to the Vineyard would be five to eight dollars. Sightseeing buses were available, and "hard surfaced roads encircled [the] island."

These words come from the *WPA Guide to Massachusetts*. In the midst of the Depression, President Roosevelt established the Federal Writers' Project to compile local and oral histories, children's books, ethnographies and other works to provide jobs for teachers, historians, librarians, writers and other white-collar workers. Eventually, about 6,600 people were employed in the project. Of all the works produced, the best known was the American Guide Series: forty-eight state guides to America, as well as the Alaska Territory, Washington, D.C., and Puerto Rico.

The Massachusetts Guide included maps, illustrations and general information. Under the title of *Main Street and Village Green*, forty-seven Massachusetts towns, villages and cities were listed, with nary a word about the Vineyard until page 554. Martha's Vineyard is eventually noted as "Tour #14 From New Bedford–Martha's Vineyard–Nantucket."

The reported tour to the Vineyard was via a thirty-five-mile ferry run from New Bedford that passed through Buzzards Bay and Woods Hole. The guide provided travelers with a description of the Vineyard that speculates Leif Ericson may have preceded Bartholomew Gosnold as the first white man to visit the island, back in 1602. The year-round resident population in 1930 was 4,963, as compared to 18,783 today.[6]

The guidebook was written just a few years before World War II and served as an introduction to the domain of Martha's Vineyard during the Depression era. Martha's Vineyard was a much different place then. Up-island was remote, removed and without electricity. Transportation was limited to dirt roads, and communication was restricted to the few people with telephones. "Until the outbreak of the war, the Vineyard remained an undiscovered country, distant, self-reliant, and ungoverned by mainland thinking. In memory and outlook, it was a place away, apart and alone, its spirit still more rooted in the nineteenth century than the twentieth."[7]

The war brought major changes to the island, both military and civilian. Our story will provide an all-encompassing historical perspective about World War II on Martha's Vineyard.

CHAPTER 1
THE ROAD TO WAR: 1940

Adolf Hitler, chancellor and dictator of Nazi Germany, ordered troops of the Third Reich to attack Poland on September 1, 1939, ostensibly because of the trumped-up Gleiwitz incident.[8] That precipitated World War II.

The following May, Nazi forces invaded Holland and Belgium and forced a third of a million British soldiers to evacuate Dunkirk, France, with a massive gathering of all sorts of boats. By the spring of 1940, Britain and the United States realized Hitler would attack them next.

Winston Churchill succeeded Neville Chamberlain as prime minister of Britain and rallied his countrymen with a series of speeches that declared England would never surrender. President Franklin D. Roosevelt gave a fireside chat in which he sought to prepare the United States for war by converting a peacetime economy to the manufacture of military munitions.

The Nazis conquered France in June 1940 and began bombing Britain in July. Six hundred German bombers blitzed London in September; four hundred people died that first night, and London sustained constant bombardment for two months.

In October 1940, the first peacetime draft was instituted in the United States with a lottery for men ages twenty-one to thirty-five; some six thousand men were called up. To meet the needs of the expanding army, army camps were hastily constructed across the country, primarily along the coasts and in the South. On Cape Cod, Camp Edwards underwent a vast expansion for incoming recruits.

Prime Minister Churchill sought fifty destroyers from the United States in return for the lease of nine British military bases. Congress approved the lend-lease bill to support Britain with munitions but kept the United States out of war. President Roosevelt ordered the manufacture of fifty thousand planes.

In early 1941, Roosevelt was inaugurated to an unprecedented third term. He urged Americans to unite with the Allied cause to secure freedom of speech and worship and freedom from want and fear. This became known as FDR's Four Freedoms speech.

"With new army camps and defense plants appearing all across the country, with textile mills running double shifts to fill orders for uniforms and blankets, with shipyards working round the clock, the unemployment rolls were swiftly shrinking...The eleven-year depression was, at last, coming to an end."[9]

Hitler invaded Russia in June 1941, and Russian leader Joseph Stalin requested arms and aluminum from the Allies to build fighter planes. Like Churchill, Stalin made it clear he would not surrender. A national scrap metal drive was initiated in America, and people began collecting old pots, pans and household metal to garner enough aluminum to make two thousand planes. The United States, Russia and Britain began to gear up for war with the manufacture of weapons and armaments.

Martha's Vineyard may have been a target for Germany when the Nazis considered an invasion of North America. Germany established an embassy in Fayal, in the Azores, with the intent to use it as a refueling station for planes headed west. One of the first sites in the eastern United States was Martha's Vineyard. The Vineyard offered a link to mainland America, with the potential for subsequent attacks.

In the late summer of 1941, President Roosevelt left Washington, ostensibly to cruise Buzzards Bay. On August 4, 1941, his private yacht, the *Potomac*, headed to Martha's Vineyard, where Roosevelt was transferred to the cruiser *Augusta* and sailed for Newfoundland to meet Churchill. The result was the Atlantic Charter, a bond of mutual support between England and the United States.

Government involvement with the citizenry expanded as war approached. The Office of Price Administration controlled what consumers paid for essential goods. The Office of Civilian Defense enlisted community volunteers as auxiliary firemen, air raid wardens and medical aides. First Lady Eleanor Roosevelt, niece of Teddy Roosevelt and wife of Franklin, joined the Office of Civilian Defense.

In November 1941, Congress amended the Neutrality Act to arm merchant ships; the United States was willing to go to war to protect ocean transport. Blackout curtains were installed in the White House, and a tunnel to the Treasury Department offered shelter, should the need arise. Washington was preparing for war.

Awareness of an escalating world war still did not convince Americans to enter the conflict. The belief, in 1940 and 1941, was that this was a European war and Americans should remain neutral or uninvolved. "It would take the attack on Pearl Harbor to create the patriotic mood that, along with rationing and a limited supply of civilian goods, stimulated Americans" to acknowledge the inevitable conflict with Nazi Germany.[10] "Gradually, one step at a time, the war was brought home to the American people."[11]

The *Vineyard Gazette* offered its version of what was happening on island: "Although nothing official has been announced, it is learned on good authority that US Army engineers have been making a survey of certain parts of Gay Head and Cuttyhunk within the past week, with a view to establishing suitable locations for fortifications should they be needed." The *Gazette* noted that this survey was a "provision against some emergency which may or may not arise."[12]

CHAPTER 2

PROTECTION AND FORTIFICATIONS

An observation station at Peaked Hill was manned by soldiers from the U.S. Army Signal Corps. The "detail is directly connected with the tests now in process, to determine the effectiveness of coastal defense against air invasion,"[13] the *Gazette* reported.

Plans for the defense of harbors along the eastern seaboard began in the mid-1930s. Martha's Vineyard was initially placed in the New Bedford district. Concrete bunkers were built at strategic shoreline sites on Martha's Vineyard and nearby islands to protect the coast from enemy ships. Spotters were stationed in the bunkers with communication lines to report enemy submarines or planes.

The initial intent of the Eastern Defense Command (EDC) was to defend harbors from Portland to New York. At its height, the EDC spanned the coastline from Greenland and Newfoundland to Bermuda and Pensacola, Florida.[14]

Minefields were laid in harbor entrances by the mine-planter *Baird* to curtail German submarines in New England waters. Submarine nets were emplaced. The Harbor Defense system was designed to meet a possible attack by the "fast and powerful motor torpedo boat."[15] From their experience in the First World War, Americas were well aware of the murderous capability of German U-boats.

Bob Tilton of Vineyard Haven was twelve years old when the war started. He remembers a group of navy servicemen in Vineyard Haven harbor called "Captain of the Port," responsible for harbor security. "They had an office right near what is now the Coastwise Wharf where the Black Dog runs its

Concrete bunkers were erected on Cuttyhunk. These camouflaged fortifications were used by soldiers to scan the waters of Vineyard Sound for U-boats. *Photo by Thomas Dresser.*

The bunker at Gay Head (now Aquinnah) now serves as an observation deck overlooking the Elizabeth Islands. A second bunker, nearby, tumbled into the sea and is barely visible below the Gay Head lighthouse. *Photo by Thomas Dresser.*

charters. Four 'crash boats' could be deployed at a moment's notice to rescue any planes in case they went down. Fortunately, they weren't used often."

———

A key defense of the homeland was establishment of beach patrols along two thousand miles of New England coast. "From fall of 1942 to fall of 1943 the patrol of large sections of the beaches was assumed by the coast guard."[16] The goal was "to protect America's shores from landings by unfriendly individuals or groups whose purpose might be to destroy or cripple the nation."[17] Protective preparation was underway.

Miles of telephone line were laid along beaches, and reporting stations were set at quarter-mile intervals. On Martha's Vineyard, Coast Guardsmen walked the beaches, especially along the extensive south shore. "New lookout towers were constructed on Martha's Vineyard at Watcha Pond, Chilmark Beach, Katama Point and Wasque Point."[18]

John Alley remembers the call boxes. "If something happened, the Shore Patrol would go to the next call box. The call boxes were all numbered. These poles and call boxes were located all along the south shore, from Gay Head to Edgartown. There was a place in Quansoo."

On Chappaquiddick, a house with a tower that overlooked the Wasque shoreline was taken by the coast guard. Bill Hannah was stationed at this facility, now known as Wasque Watch. "His detail was to patrol the beach there."[19] Fifteen to twenty-five men were stationed there, searching for German U-boats that might put men ashore. In addition, farmhouses were appropriated by the coast guard in Squibnocket and Quansoo.[20] A coast guardsman used a shed in Menemsha to

This private house on Chappaquiddick was appropriated by the U.S. Coast Guard during the war. Two dozen men were stationed at what was affectionately known as the Chappy Hilton. *Photo by Thomas Dresser.*

monitor fishing boats moving in and out of the harbor.

Coast guardsmen patrolled the shoreline around Gay Head, monitored telephones and rescued boaters. Coast guard vehicles patrolled the road above the Chilmark cliffs at Windy Gates, day and night, searching for saboteurs who might land from German submarines.

Young coast guardsmen became the face of the war for local residents. Jane Slater recalls, "At Squibnocket, the coast guard had a sub-station at a farmhouse. They had men to patrol the beaches. At the beginning, they patrolled singly, then double, and still later they had dogs.[21] And they would drive their Jeep down to the post office." Protection provided by the coast guard on tiny Martha's Vineyard was integral to the defense of the nation as a whole.

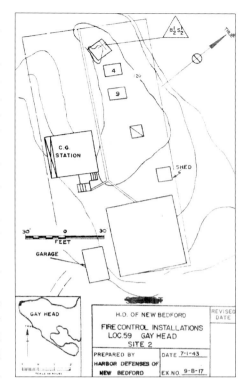

Coast guard headquarters was at Gay Head during the war, near the Gay Head lighthouse. Commander Howard Johnson was in charge. *Courtesy of Mark Berlow.*

Another Chilmark resident, Nancy Nitchie, recalls, "The war came when I was eleven. My family shielded me from a lot of the war news. The coast guard walked around the island. They had a place they walked to see if anything came in or washed up on the beach."

Key Post Corner is a specific site on Nantucket. As Jean Allen described it, "Coast guard men patrolled the perimeter of the whole island on foot, around the clock. As the men passed different 'key posts' around the island, they had to punch in on a time clock. They wore the 'key' around their neck, and should they be late punching in, the worst was to be suspected—that somewhere a German sub had landed, preventing the check-in."[22]

Jane Slater, a teenager during the war, empathized with the young men, who were only a few years older than herself. "Those poor young men that patrolled the beach. Never seen the ocean before, not familiar with the sound of the waves; they must have been terrified." She adds, "They patrolled twenty-four hours. There was so much real and imagined fear among the soldiers. The people who lived here weren't afraid. We didn't know what it was all about, so we weren't afraid. It was so exciting."

Coastal defense was designed "to insure [sic] use of waterways between Long Island Sound and Buzzard's [sic] Bay secure from enemy naval gun fire and cover the debouchment (movement from narrow to wider opening) by our fleet into the Atlantic Ocean." Ships leaving port were vulnerable as they ventured into the open sea. The goal was "to protect harbor facilities and friendly vessels in Narragansett Bay from enemy naval gun fire."[23]

Coastal defense leased land for bunkers and installations on the Elizabeth Islands. "Two coastal defense units were constructed by the Army on the higher points of Naushon for submarine surveillance with a detachment of 6 to 8 men each."[24] On Cuttyhunk, in addition to three bunkers, a Fire Control Station (antiaircraft guns), radar, housing and battery site were erected by July 1943. And in Woods Hole, wooden barracks were erected on Juniper Point.

Military installations and concrete bunkers were camouflaged to avoid detection. "All barracks, administrative buildings, and other structures on government owned or controlled land will be painted of such color as to blend in with the surrounding buildings and terrain,"[25] according to War Department regulations. The concrete bunkers along the shoreline blended into the clay cliffs of Gay Head.

The Signal Service of the EDC, working with Bell Telephone Company, devised an Aircraft Warning Service with communication systems, information centers and observation posts. Protection of the shoreline improved immeasurably during the war with use of radar in conjunction with torpedo boat weapons, which tracked submarines at sea and bombers aloft. A fire control tower served as antiaircraft protection. While personal observation was required at the onset of the war, radar and improved anti-submarine armaments proved successful in combating German U-boats as the war went on.

On Cape Cod, Camp Edwards was expanded. "This was the first such camp building project undertaken for World War II. Methods and lessons learned here were carried throughout the country as all the other military posts built their 'temporary' war-time buildings."[26] In the fall of 1941, the Twenty-sixth Yankee Infantry Division of Massachusetts National Guard arrived at Camp Edwards.

CHAPTER 3

THE ATLANTIC CHARTER: 1941

President Roosevelt sought legislation from Congress to furnish supplies and military equipment to Great Britain. Leaders with the dedication, intelligence and stature of General George C. Marshal and Admiral Ernest J. King led the United States in preparation for war.

A series of events took place in the life of President Roosevelt, beginning on August 2, 1941, which had an impact on the world stage. And these events involved Martha's Vineyard. On that day, President Roosevelt boarded his presidential yacht *Potomac*, but neither the press nor the secret service, supposedly, knew where the president was headed.

"Today, it couldn't happen. But in August 1941 it did. The press didn't know where the President of the United States was! Supposedly he was on a holiday cruise, avoiding the oppressive heat and humidity of Washington, aboard the presidential yacht *Potomac*."[27]

President Roosevelt had a deep love of the sea. From his days as assistant secretary of the navy, he chose not to be extravagant with elegant appointments aboard ship. Since stricken with polio in 1921 at the age of thirty-nine, FDR was a paraplegic. His fear of fire was intense, so he had a hand-operated elevator installed in a false smokestack on the *Potomac*. On his cruises, recreation consisted of fishing, poker and chatting with family and friends, activities he appreciated when not engrossed by his beloved stamp collection.

In a presidential letter to his cousin Margaret "Daisy" Suckley, FDR documented staging his escape from Washington without the knowledge of his ever-present press corps: "It was constantly emphasized, both in London and Washington, that the utmost secrecy before and during the trip was essential."[28] A bomb from a German plane or torpedo from a German submarine was a very real threat even before the United States entered the war.

He continued: "I then remembered that I had told my Press Conference about ten days before that I needed to get off for a cruise on the USS *Potomac* to the eastern coast of Maine in order to get some cool nights—the summer of 1941 being extremely hot in June and July. This became the basis for the plan of escape."[29]

The *Vineyard Gazette* shared a scoop: "While mainland newspapers and radio scouts hunted in vain, to use their own expression, for President Roosevelt on Tuesday and Tuesday night, the Chief Executive was lying snugly and quietly aboard the *Potomac* anchored in Tarpaulin Cove" off Naushon island. Very few people knew the presidential yacht was in Vineyard waters. The *Gazette* added, "But so far as is known no one attempted to approach the craft and certainly no one who knew of her presence there, tipped off any institution or individual that might have invaded her privacy."[30]

Ann Barry, age sixteen, recalled that day: "A distinct memory I have is watching FDR's private ship, the *Potomac*, as it positioned itself in the bay of Menemsha. It was moored quite close to the shoreline. There were other surrounding ships nearby which we later learned had a standby status to protect the president."

Ann and her cousins were curious about the vessel and decided to row out to investigate. As they approached the ship, she said, "armed guards on the boat trained their guns in our direction. Evidently they thought our little armada of rowboats posed a threat. Even though we didn't understand the gravity of that visit and who was on board, it was still pretty impressive to us."

The *Potomac* was accompanied by the cruiser *Augusta* and six destroyers: *Tuscaloosa, Madison, Moffett, Sampson, Winslow* and *McDougal*.

The *Gazette* report continued: "Menemsha residents rubbed their eyes in amazement, yesterday afternoon, when six warships loomed up on the horizon shortly after noon, as they approached within a mile of the beach and anchored."[31]

No one knew what was going on. Sailboats and rowboats circled the waters but could not ascertain the purpose of the visit. Even a sailor aboard one of the ships appeared befuddled, as he queried onlookers as to his location.

On August 4, 1941, British prime minister Winston Churchill secretly left England on the warship *Prince of Wales*, headed for Argentia, Newfoundland. "The suggestion to meet at what would later be called the Atlantic Conference had come from the prime minister. Hoping to involve the United States more deeply in the struggle against Hitler, Churchill sought to prepare a joint declaration of war aims."[32]

"The *Potomac* continued on her holiday cruise, pulling into Tarpaulin Cove for a restful afternoon and overnight anchorage."[33] The next day, the *Potomac* headed through the Cape Cod Canal; sightseers along the canal assumed it was President Roosevelt and his staff they saw on deck. The *Potomac* continued to send messages about fish caught and relaxation enjoyed, ostensibly by the president, though he was far away.

Although the men on the deck of the *Potomac* enjoyed the breezes off Buzzards Bay and the presidential ensign still proudly flew, President Roosevelt was not aboard ship. The president had disembarked from the *Potomac* and boarded the cruiser *Augusta*, which steamed north, far from the curious citizens of Vineyard Sound.

President Roosevelt recorded an account of his adventure: "After time in Non quit [*sic*], we reversed course and, going around the south end of Cuddyhunk [*sic*] Island, we anchored in the midst of seven US Warships at about 11 pm at Menemsha Bight on the western end of Martha's Vineyard." The ships were darkened for protection. At dawn, the *Potomac* came alongside the *Augusta*, and the president and his retinue transferred to the larger vessel.

As the president recounted by letter, "And then, the Island of Martha's Vineyard disappeared in the distance, and as we head out into the Atlantic...Curiously enough the *Potomac* still flies my flag and tonight will be seen by thousands as she passes quietly through the Cape Cod Canal...Even at my ripe old age, I feel a thrill in making a get-away—especially from the American press. It is a smooth sea & a lovely day."[34]

Roosevelt added, "Captain Leahy had dressed four or five of his crew in civilian clothes and had them sit on the after deck pretending to be the President and his party." The president met up with two of his sons, Franklin Jr. and Elliott, en route to Newfoundland; neither knew their father was on a secret mission.

In Newfoundland, Roosevelt and Churchill spent three days working out an agreement whereby the United States would support the Allied forces against German aggression. This resulted in the signing of the Atlantic Charter, which took place under auspicious circumstances.

Henry Beetle Hough described his role: "We did not learn until later that Washington had made some sort of request for secrecy about the President's goings and comings—certainly no such request had come to us."[35]

The *Gazette* explained, "Roosevelt had evaded his ever-present guard of wire service reporters, leaving behind a faint look-alike to lounge smoking on the afterdeck and wave grandly at sailors who cruised nearby under the watchful eye of a Coast Guard cutter." And that explains why the six warships were anchored off Menemsha. President Roosevelt had not spent the night "snugly and quietly aboard the *Potomac* anchored in Tarpaulin Cove," as the *Gazette* had reported. "Too bad—FDR would have loved Tarpaulin Cove."[36]

President Roosevelt's Vineyard visit lives on in local lore. Nancy Nitchie recalls, "We knew about Roosevelt meeting Churchill in Canada." She goes on: "Roosevelt was overnight between the Vineyard and the Elizabeth Islands. We knew it was FDR. Don't know how we knew. People on the Vineyard knew. Another group of ships came by. It was very exciting. My family knew this more than me."

CHAPTER 4

COLONEL LINDBERGH

Colonel Charles Lindbergh and his family rented a house in West Tisbury, at Seven Gates Farm, from August 1941 through May 1942. "They were people who wanted privacy," Helen Duarte, their cook, said. "They made that clear."[37] Lindbergh sought to avoid the celebrity status that accompanied him following his nonstop, solo transatlantic flight in 1927 and the kidnapping of his son Charles in 1932.

In 1938, Lindbergh reviewed Nazi aircraft and received a medal of honor from Hermann Goering, founder of the Gestapo and commander of the Luftwaffe (German air force). Lindbergh became spokesman for the America First Committee, an isolationist group with some 800,000 members. Many in the press and public considered Lindbergh an appeaser as he argued against President Roosevelt's foreign policy. In an effort to avoid the backlash that accompanied such publicity, Colonel Lindbergh sought refuge on Martha's Vineyard.

In a letter to her mother, Anne Morrow Lindbergh, Charles's wife, wrote, "I do not feel so overcome up here…no telephone calls, no people, no dates ahead. I feel deliciously lonely and hope I stay so!" Colonel Lindbergh recorded in his journal that Martha's Vineyard was "quiet, stimulating, inspiring."[38]

Lindbergh arrived on the Vineyard with his pregnant wife, three children, two secretaries, a governess and a chambermaid. He hired Duarte as his cook, as well as her husband, Maynard. Anne Morrow Lindbergh reviewed each day's menu. "I was glad because I was a little nervous at first," Helen

Duarte said. "I'd phone the order in to SBS, which was a grocery store then near the harbor. Then my husband would go and pick it up. They never expected anything fancy. They were meat, potatoes and vegetable persons." Duarte added, "On Martha's Vineyard everybody is so friendly and kind, and I found that out more and more as time went by."

Anne Morrow was an acclaimed poet who wrote in a large tent "way out in the woods," according to Helen Duarte. The colonel's activities were a mystery. "What he did I couldn't tell you," she said. "He would come in the kitchen a lot. He was a great walker and used to go off-Island a lot. Then he'd have dark glasses and wear his hat down, as if in disguise."[39]

In the spring of 1942, Charles Lindbergh abruptly moved his family off island. By then, he fully supported the war. Lindbergh became a test pilot, invented a cruise-control device to aid fighter pilots and flew more than fifty combat missions in the Pacific theater.

That Charles Lindbergh and his family hid out on Martha's Vineyard was not unknown to the local press. Henry Beetle Hough and his wife, Betty, "knew a news story when they saw one, but they no doubt chose not to print anything about the Lindberghs out of respect for their privacy."[40]

CHAPTER 5

CIVILIAN DEFENSE

A year before the bombing of Pearl Harbor, three young men from Martha's Vineyard enlisted in the military. They thought that if they enlisted then, in December 1940, they would get out sooner or they would rise in rank, getting a head start on their peers. In any case, Francis Fisher[41] and Hobart Willoughby of Edgartown and Basil Look of Oak Bluffs enlisted at Local 173 in the Legion Hall[42] in Vineyard Haven and were inducted into the United States Army, the first Vineyarders to enlist in World War II.

With congressional approval of the Selective Service Act in mid-1941, men ages twenty to forty-five were required to register with their draft board. The *Vineyard Gazette* reported that twelve men registered in Tisbury, fourteen in Oak Bluffs, seven in Edgartown, three in West Tisbury, one each in Chilmark and Gosnold and no one in Gay Head. The sole registrant from Gosnold, on Cuttyhunk, was actually a resident of Vineyard Haven "whose card was brought to Vineyard Haven by the coast guard, this being the only way that it could be obtained in time for filing."[43]

Many people realized that war with Germany was inevitable. Those who had witnessed the devastation of the First World War knew Hitler would attempt to conquer all of Europe as revenge for Germany's capitulation in the earlier conflict.

President Roosevelt began to prepare the civilian population for war. The practical element was: know what to do in the event of an attack. The psychological element encouraged everyone to feel like part of the war effort. Both aspects of civilian defense were key to secure the homeland.

Preparation for a potential bombing attack encompassed behavioral changes. Air raid drills were coordinated by wardens in each town, supplemented by auxiliary police and firemen. Blackouts were imposed to eliminate light from houses and roadways. Light could silhouette ships along the shore, making them a target for attack by German U-boats. State guards were organized to provide a physical presence.

War in Europe was a reality. Awareness of the Battle of Britain made it conceivable that enemy planes could bomb Martha's Vineyard. German submarines patrolled the waters offshore. An effort was underway to show how prepared and resilient the population was.

Connie Frank remembers how the Vineyard was changing as war loomed on the horizon: "The harbor and the traffic out of town was very crowded with many military trucks and vans loaded with soldiers and endless equipment heading up to begin and maintain Peaked Hill."

————

A local headline read: "Vineyard Tests its Strength in Mock Bombing Raids." Civilians were to "show how they could defend their community against the demoralization and damage of bombing."[44] A simulated disaster cut off the water supply and disrupted communication. Warnings were issued that planes were about to bomb the Vineyard. Reports were sent to Civilian Defense offices to dispatch equipment and personnel. The Vineyard actively participated in this mock bombing raid.

As part of the exercise, schools were evacuated and children hid in the nearby woods to prepare for an emergency. In Chilmark, schoolchildren got wet feet playing in a nearby stream. "We were at school," recalls Bud Mayhew. "Teacher said the word that there were German bombers, and so they sent us home and they said, 'Don't go home by the roads, go through the woods.'" In Edgartown, "a number of children [were] turning up two days later with ivy poisoning."[45]

Stella "Peachie" (Leighton) Dawley, a teenager at the Edgartown School, recalls "a bell signal that sounded in the school indicating an air raid drill had just started." Students filed out. "The students were instructed to go into the cornfield with the high cornstalks and hide so they couldn't be seen. They had to remain in that field until the 'all clear' signal bell was sounded by the school officials."

Additionally, fire and police departments across the island participated. A simulated bombing of a house played out. The Martha's Vineyard Hospital exhibited appropriate preparation. One mishap occurred when the bell rope of Trinity Church snapped as the alarm first sounded, but by and large, the "mock raids [were] carried out with good humor, but with underlying earnestness."[46] These actions were taken six weeks before the attack at Pearl Harbor.

"The first practice blackout of the Martha's Vineyard Hospital went off well, with the prospect that the hospital will be in readiness in any cases of air raid emergency," reported the *Gazette*. The paper advised that in an actual air raid, it is imperative to shut off gas, fill a bathtub with water and keep a window open.

Week by week, training of Civilian Defense personnel and citizenry on the island improved as the nation prepared for the inevitability of war.

CHAPTER 6

WAR

Nancy Swift worked at the Van Ryper model shop in Vineyard Haven. The entry in her diary of December 7, 1941, reads:

Today went to Priscilla's [West]. Was waiting for her to get ready to go out. News reports coming over radio about Japs attacking Hawaii (Pearl Harbor). Surprised. Went to Jeannette's Dinette. Ernie and the cook there, talking about it, and from then on we heard about it from everyone who came in. It dazed me. We looked at our friends in a different light. Soon they would be leaving.

Came home. All we heard was news reports cutting in on regular programs. Went to bed with news flashes ringing in my ears and woke up hearing them, for that is all you can find on the radio. I woke up feeling sick, chilled and excited. I finally realized what this really means. The more you think about it the more you feel. All I can think about is the fellows my age, the kids in our graduating class last June, who will be going. I felt like bawling. I remember the tears in the eyes at our graduation when Nellie Bryant delivered his commencement address and alluded to what the future of this class would be. I remember the tears running down George Sears' cheeks. And now it had come.

Swift[47] captured the emotions of that fateful day. Her words resonate decades later: "Listened to Pres. Roosevelt's speech in Beanie's [Alley] car at noontime behind the Post Office. Certainly made us see how serious it was and we realized we were really going to see our first World War. Got back to Shop, listened to House and Senate voting. WE ARE AT WAR."

———

Donald Billings of Oak Bluffs says:

> *I remember that day like it was today. I was at Dr. Gunn's office, upstairs above what is now Mocha Motts. We were playing Monopoly and going to listen to the* Shadow *program on the radio. It was interrupted by an announcement about the war. Dr. Gunn sent us kids home, saying, "Your parents will be worried about you." We listened to President Roosevelt on the radio. Didn't really know what it meant.*

———

The *Vineyard Gazette* reported the onset of war: "A tremor of mixed excitement and dread swept the Vineyard on Sunday when the first news of the Japanese attack in the Pacific Islands became known through radio broadcasts."[48] The news brought the war home, hard and fast, although the bombing was halfway around the world. Vineyarders felt the same anguish as communities across the country.

Pearl Harbor proved a boon for enlistment. Men registered and were inducted. Uniforms were ordered. War was no longer a future fear but a present reality. A *Gazette* editorial remarked on the patriotic activities of the young men of the island. "It is pretty impressive the way so many Island boys, those who were romping around in a carefree fashion not so long ago, have taken to responsibility in the Army, or the Navy, or the Marines."[49] By the spring of 1942, however, a second age group was called up, a draft of "old men," as the *Gazette* referred to them, those between the ages of forty-five and sixty-five. This drew 526 "old boys" from the Vineyard populace.

Those who could volunteered to serve in the military and did so with pride. Within six months of the bombing of Pearl Harbor, 40 percent of American citizens volunteered in some way. From Martha's Vineyard, 12 percent of the people served: 677 veterans out of the 1940 census of 5,669. On nearby Nantucket, 495 served out of a population of 3,400.

CHAPTER 7

THE HOMEFRONT: 1942

That year, 1942, was the low water mark for America in World War II with the United States at its lowest point.[50]

Citizens were encouraged to become part of the nationwide war effort. Civilian Defense expanded air raid drills, and wardens volunteered to oversee the exercises. Blackout drills were held. Local communities were eager to get involved.

To coordinate the efforts of citizens, the federal government enacted multiple programs, regulations and requests to involve the citizenry. The result was that virtually everyone participated and contributed. It was considered patriotic to sacrifice on the homefront to support the men and women in the armed forces.

Dorothy Bunker recalled that "the campground was shrouded in fear but sometimes lit by humor during the dark war years." Elderly neighbors could pose a challenge when they did not understand blackout restrictions. Her story unfolded as she and her neighbor became air raid wardens for Wesleyan Grove Camp Meeting Association in Oak Bluffs. "Everyone rushed to do his duty, with the fear of Germans bombing from airplanes or lurking offshore in submarines."

Air raid sirens were common. "When the alarm sounded, they never were sure whether the raid was real or not," Bunker said.

A memorable practice air raid began with flour scattered by the entrance to the campground to signify an attack. "Mr. Peters, eighty years or more, was the preordained victim, lying within his cottage." Rescuers hurried in and put him on their stretcher; "however, being burdened with their patient, they found there was no way to rush the stretcher out of the narrow campground cottage doorway. So Mr. Peters obligingly got up and walked out the door to resume his prone position." The ambulance, a plumbing truck, was not quite long enough for Mr. Peters. "Dot recalls old Mr. Peters' good natured head hanging out the back end of the truck and bumping off, being rushed to the Martha's Vineyard Hospital, trying hard not to laugh." After a practice raid, wardens gravitated to Charlie Friller's drugstore on Circuit Avenue for ice cream sundaes and to share their adventures.[51]

Bud Mayhew recalled an incident up-island: "Civilian Defense went around. There was an exercise. They put us Chilmark kids—and there weren't that many of us—down at Nab's Corner, in the woods, and each of us had a different injury." The mock victims were brought down to the Marine Hospital in Vineyard Haven but "not by ambulance, as they didn't use ambulances up here in Chilmark. And they put us up on the operating table. It was the Civilian Defense people."

Helen (Viera) Gelotte recalled her role as a telephone operator in Vineyard Haven during air raids: "They were done with the fire alarm blasting. There was a big clock, and you stuck in a gear that told where the fire was. Each number signaled a different location, like #21 was on Main Street. Everybody knew what each number meant. It was very scary when it went off. The air raid signal was three."

The local Civilian Defense Committee issued detailed instructions on what to do when the signal sounded. Among suggestions was, "Don't create panic." The memo urged people to stay inside or, if away from home, not to mingle with crowds. Above all, they should remain calm. The population was advised that "the duties of civilians are as vital to the country's welfare as are those of the armed forces."

German U-boats used backlighting of coastal cities and towns to attack ships. A vessel's silhouette could be highlighted by light from behind the ship, hence the imposition of blackouts. Local Civilian Defense wardens checked that house lights were extinguished or dark curtains blocked light. Beyond the practical goal of eliminating targets for German submarines and bombers, blackouts reminded people that the country was at war. Compliance was linked to patriotism, integral to victory.

Window shades were made of Sisalcraft paper, impermeable to light. Amid all the dire warnings, the official position was that, inside, the house should remain cheery.

Freeman Leonard explained, "We, on the Vineyard, were 'blacked out' for military purposes. This meant no lights were allowed at night, which could provide possible bombing targets for our enemies." He went on: "Fortunately, I knew most of the roads, but, when in doubt, I rigged a small spotlight which cast a beam as big around as your finger. It safely guided me along the side of the road."[52]

"I remember it clearly as my brother stood on the running board of our car as we traveled back to Chilmark," recalls Ann Barry. "He shined a flashlight on the middle of the road's white line to keep us to the right. We had to go very slowly, hoping no other cars were coming toward us."

In an editorial, the *Gazette* sought to bolster morale by noting the lack of a military target or industry on the island, which meant that there was no reason it should be bombed. "In short, it seems to us that this Island, far from being undefended, is defended very well indeed, and we may well be satisfied to have the available anti-aircraft batteries placed around congested areas and military and industrial centers. We do not need them."[53]

Gazette editor Henry Beetle Hough debunked the idea that the Vineyard was a military target; the island was too bucolic, not worthy of enemy bombs. General Ennis, head of Civilian Defense, added, "I do not believe any enemy would attack Martha's Vineyard as a major objective."[54] This allayed fear, but towns still ran practice drills. Oak Bluffs planned a blackout drill on January 11, 1942. Air raid wardens checked that curtains were drawn. The partial blackout was deemed a success. Only five houses failed to comply due to misunderstanding the import of the drill or being unaware it was taking place.

Edgartown followed with a blackout, but no restrictions were placed on automobile traffic. Although the thermometer dropped to six degrees, West Tisbury held a blackout. The air raid warning siren sounded in town, and church bells rang in Lambert's Cove and North and West Tisbury.

Betty Honey, a Vineyard Haven air raid warden, recalled, "All of a sudden you'd be aroused by 'Zoom, zoom, zoom, zoom!' Me, still in school, I am out there with an armband, going around every house, looking for light." Betty was organized, making a chart and checking off each house. "It was pitch black everywhere, and I had a flashlight with a piece of cardboard and a pinhole in it, just enough so I could see where I was going."[55]

Ruth Stiller remembers, "My brother had to get up in the middle of the night and walk Main Street in Vineyard Haven. He checked on the blackouts for each of the homes. He would also go to Gay Head if someone had a ride for him. He'd go in that cement bunker up there or go to South Beach with his binoculars to make sure there were no subs."

Teenagers, too, were involved in Civilian Defense, recalls Robert Bigelow. "Living in West Chop, I patrolled from my house partway to Vineyard Haven. I was only a kid, part of the Civilian Defense during high school years. Up and down streets. Report anything curious. Double-checking things. Don't recall anything suspicious. Everybody was encouraging me."

In May 1942, banker Stephen Carey Luce Jr. replaced retired General William Ennis as coordinator for Civilian Defense. Luce's goal was to boost morale and improve discipline.

An island-wide blackout was held on July 8, 1942. "The Island was darkened, according to regulations,"[56] and inspected from the air. Island coordinator Luce was pleased with the response.

Doris Gregory first visited the Vineyard in 1944 with her future mother-in-law. Coming from Chicago, she was amazed at the strict blackout adhered to on the Vineyard, with headlights half-covered, dim streetlights and dark green window shades that emitted no house light. Walking though Edgartown, it was so dark she could not see her way. Her experience in Chicago was that the war did not mean as much as it did on Martha's Vineyard.

Eventually, regulations on night driving were eased. "Car headlights had to block off the top half," Bud Mayhew remembers, "and when you come up a hill, like Abel's Hill, you'd put on the parking lights because you didn't want the German subs to see the lights." The rest of the island used parking lights and traveled only fifteen miles per hour.

Driving rules were relaxed because, said Frank Goodwin, state registrar for Martha's Vineyard, "there is far more danger of killing people with automobiles when the drivers cannot see where they are going than there is from submarines."[57]

The Massachusetts Committee on Public Safety sought to designate certain structures as air raid shelters. "We have been requested under date of September 23rd [1942] to ascertain the location of any buildings in your town that would be suitable for an Air Raid Shelter in case of bombing." Aerial bombing was considered a possibility.

Civilian Defense director Luce appointed Sergeant Altieri of the state police to be the Vineyard's air raid shelter and bomb inspector. Altieri had recently completed course work at the War Department and Civilian Defense School in New Bedford. He was authorized to select air raid shelters and determine appropriate equipment.

In Edgartown, the Catholic Church and Hall's Elm Theater granted approval for their sites as shelters. The prominent, columned Methodist church, the Old Whaling Church, would not serve as a shelter, as it was deemed "a sufficient bombing target in an air raid to preclude its usefulness as a shelter." On Nantucket, the dome of the Unitarian Church was painted black.

Following is a list of designated Edgartown air raid shelters:

WARDENS REPORT FORM	
ISLAND OF MARTHA'S VINEYARD	

Commence with the words "AIR RAID DAMAGE"

WARDENS SECTOR NUMBER

LOCATION OF DAMAGE

TYPE OF BOMBS.   H.E. ☐   Incendiary ☐   Poison Gas ☐

Approx. No. of Casualties
(If any trapped under wreckage, say so)

If Fire, say so

Damage to Mains.   Water ☐   Gas ☐   Electric ☐   Sewers ☐

Names of Roads Blocked

Position of Unexploded Bombs

Time of Bombing (approx.)

Services already on Spot

Remarks

Finish with the words "End of Message"

ORIGINAL   These words are for use with a report sent by
DUPLICATE   messenger.
            Delete whichever does not apply.

This form was to be completed if Martha's Vineyard were ever bombed. It was never used. *Courtesy of Martha's Vineyard Museum.*

- Catholic Chapel on Pease's Point Way and High Street
- Edgartown School gym
- County Jail
- Congregational Church
- Catholic Church
- County courthouse
- Episcopal Church
- Public library
- Elm Theatre

Air raid wardens distributed precautions and warnings. When the siren blew, people were to get off the street, into a nearby building and away from windows. Unnecessary automobile driving was forbidden. Advice on how to extinguish an incendiary bomb was to not spray it, as it would explode; one should use sandbags instead.

Island schools faced the war. In his 1943 annual report, Superintendent of Schools Arthur Lord wrote, "The 'all out' war effort has resulted in peace time activities of little consequence. World activities should not be the emphasis in the lives of children from six to 16. While in school world actions should be of secondary nature with his or her school activities primary."

The Oak Bluffs School "has tried to keep pace with the nation at war by continuing to adapt its program to the needs of pupils in order that they may be better prepared to meet the demands of the post-war world." The school nurse reported, "No phase of education is more important in the lives of the children of a nation at war than that which teaches them how to attain and maintain good health."[58]

In Edgartown, the principal, Walter M. Morris, and teachers Joseph P. Barry and Edward Campbell "entered the service of their country." A report noted that the three were experienced, faithful, competent and missed. The report also stated, with great satisfaction, that Brigadier General Theodore H. Dillon served as vice-principal. He was on army leave and provided the district with a leader who was respected by teachers and students.[59]

Bob Hughes joined the navy. The Oak Bluffs school report read, "It was with much regret that Mr. Hughes was released for the duration of the war. Mr. Hughes is an unusually strong teacher and we hope for his early return to the high school staff."[60]

At the onset of hostilities, in December 1941, it was determined that the American Red Cross War Fund should raise some $50 million. Local war fund chairman Captain Ralph M. Packer "alluded to destruction wrought in Hawaii and other points attacked by the Japanese"[61] in his effort to raise monies on Martha's Vineyard.

Captain Packer announced quotas for each town: Oak Bluffs and Edgartown were to raise $1,200 each; Vineyard Haven's quota was $1,350;

Jackie Baer recalled, "There were savings bonds, but you started with savings stamps. You built up these stamps, then you could get a bond if you had $18.75." *Photo by Joyce Dresser.*

Chilmark and West Tisbury had quotas set at $225 each; and Gay Head had a goal of $50. By mid-February1942, the Red Cross War Fund neared its goal of $4,250.

War bonds helped make schoolchildren aware of the war effort. "There were war bond drives," recalls Megan Alley, "and at the school each week, we would bring in our very special quarters and buy stamps to put in a booklet. When it was filled, we would take it to the bank or post office and turn it in for a savings bond."

The people of Nantucket prepared for war with sandbags against incendiary bombs. Steamships were painted gray[62] and blacked out; ferry schedules went unpublished for fear of sabotage. "Nantucket was a lonely and vulnerable place in the dark days of late 1941 and early 1942."[63]

CHAPTER 8

PLANE SPOTTERS

Following the bombing of Britain in 1940 and attack on Pearl Harbor in 1941, a very real fear arose that enemy aircraft could and would attack the continental United States. An airplane spotter program was developed, staffed by volunteers, to scan the skies for incoming enemy aircraft.

Observation posts were designated. Volunteers, from high school students to senior citizens, were trained to observe planes and log registration numbers or national insignias. Local posts were staffed around the clock in Oak Bluffs, Vineyard Haven and Edgartown.

Carol Carr's father was a plane spotter on East Chop, Oak Bluffs. "Right up by the lighthouse, there was a shack with a pot-bellied stove to keep you warm in the wintertime," she recalled. "And on the wall were posters of German planes, sideways and looking up, so you could see them from the bottom. And I used to go up and keep him company. He was one of the volunteers." Carol adds, "Everyone was so patriotic about the war and feeling that you wanted to do everything you could to help."

One young man, still in high school, volunteered as a plane spotter. Oak Bluffs senior Anthony Amaral wrote an essay that was published in the *Observation Post*. His site by the East Chop lighthouse had a tower and was equipped with a logbook, telephone and compass. Amaral noted the boats in Vineyard Sound and lights from Camp Edwards, but his primary responsibilities lay aloft, scanning the skies for aircraft and reporting any planes he saw or heard to army headquarters at Camp Edwards. On a beautiful, clear, moonlit night, he wrote, "Standing in the watch tower of the post on such a night as this, one can, for just a brief moment, forget the troubles of this grief-stricken world."[64]

"At the top of the Tisbury Association Hall [in Vineyard Haven, now the town hall] was an area for the plane spotters," says Rosalie Powell. "Behind the stage, there was a stairway up to the roof, which we climbed to reach the observation post. While up there, we studied the different silhouettes of airplanes. It was serious business for us." She went on: "We were particularly proud that we could identify the planes which flew out of the [Vineyard's] navy base airport. We could distinguish a TBF [torpedo bomber–fighter] from a Japanese TBM [torpedo bomber Mitsubishi] and the planes which folded up their wings for aircraft carriers."

Jackie Baer remembers, "Mrs. Trumper spent nights watching for enemy aircraft in the East Chop lighthouse. She had a book she carried illustrating each aircraft in silhouette." Helen Gelotte recalls "decks of cards with pictures of airplanes on them to tell the difference between an American Flying Fortress and a German Heinkel-111."

Connie Frank recollects "rushing to the windows to watch airplanes because we had never seen them before. We loved it when groups of planes came by the island."

The Edgartown observation post was on Mill Hill, off Cleavelandtown Road. Nearly fifty volunteers attained certificates in Aircraft Recognition, and six received "For Merit" medals for five-hundred-hour efforts.

In the spring of 1942, a plea was made for more plane spotters. A course in airplane identification was offered by Mrs. Alexander Orr, recognition officer of the Edgartown observation post; she had been trained by the army in New York. Work was underway on a new observation post in Edgartown.

It was reported as news in 1943 that two years prior, a plane spotter in the Royal Observer Corps had seen a German plane, piloted by Nazi Rudolph Hess, fly in over Scotland. Hess parachuted down, bearing peace proposals for a treaty between Germany and Great Britain. His effort proved futile, ignored by the British and derided by Hitler. Hess was captured and imprisoned until his death in 1987.

Abruptly, in October 1943, the War Department suspended the Aircraft Warning Service or plane spotter program. "Up to last week, the vital importance of the civilian posts was being stressed in material sent out under government auspices, and efforts were under way to obtain more spotters,"[65] the *Gazette* noted pointedly. The success of radar precluded the need for citizen airplane spotters.

Author Jay Schofield remembers that during the Cold War in the late 1950s, when he was in high school on Cape Cod, "it was common for me, along with my friends, to report to a Civil Air Patrol observation post after school. On the walls were charts of silhouettes of Russian planes. I recall that my buddies and I were excited to learn the shapes of them as we stared out the windows looking to the skies."

For Jane Slater, a young girl in Chilmark, war memories are still poignant:

I remember so vividly standing on the top of the cliffs on beautiful summer days in the early days of the War, watching convoys of ships pass the other side of Noman's going to Europe, silent, dark and foreboding. It seemed that it took all day for them to pass from sight; and I guess it did. Those same years we watched and listened to squadrons of aircraft passing over Chilmark on their way to Europe. Again, it seemed as if they were flying by for hours at a time…and they probably were. I can still hear that drone of those engines.[66]

CHAPTER 9

PEAKED HILL

B efore war broke out, there was a military presence on Martha's Vineyard. Possibly the best known World War II military encampment was the former U.S. Army Signal Corps base on what was then referred to as Peaked Hill but is known today as Radar Hill. In October 1941, the U.S. Army Signal Corps established an observation station on Peaked Hill, one of the highest points on the Vineyard, with a 360-degree view of the surrounding waters. In the 1940s, that view was unobstructed by trees.

The site was officially designated as the Peaked Hill Radar Station. Historically, however, the World War II site on the Vineyard was the signal corps' fourth deployment or involvement on Martha's Vineyard.

The United States Army Signal Corps first came to Martha's Vineyard in 1866, just after the Civil War. At that time, it installed a fifteen-mile telegraph line from Cedar Tree Neck to the Gay Head lighthouse. The line was to help the corps display cautionary signals in Gay Head and provide rescue in shipwrecks.[67] Altogether, seventy-six miles of seacoast lines were installed, which included the lines on Martha's Vineyard and from Wood's Holl (the corps' spelling) to Nantucket.[68]

Reports by the chief signal officer of the army noted many changes in the lines along the Atlantic coast, which included cable and land lines between the mainland via Martha's Vineyard to Nantucket. These lines operated without interruption and were in excellent working order.[69]

Legislation for seacoast and telegraph lines passed Congress in 1874. The act called for the operation, construction and repair of the seacoast and

Signal stations were positioned along the coastline, including Martha's Vineyard. This is a reenactment station at Camp Edwards. *Photo by Joyce Dresser.*

military telegraph lines and fell under the aegis of the chief signal officer. Although the telegraph lines were designed primarily for military use, they were available for maritime commercial use and for local residents' use.

Seacoast cables and lines connected Martha's Vineyard and Nantucket with the telegraph system in Woods Hole. The Martha's Vineyard and Nantucket lines provided telegraph communication for year-round residents and summer visitors. The lines functioned as storm-warning signals and daily weather reporting. The addition of a cable across Vineyard Sound allowed for the building of a station at Gay Head to note ships in distress, as well as counting the number that sailed the Sound annually; in one year, sixty thousand vessels passed by.

Due to a shortage of skilled signalmen, the Connecticut National Guard was involved in maneuvers with the navy and army. Connecticut was the only state to order its signal corps to participate in local maneuvers. The situation improved when two officers and men from the New York State Signal Corps volunteered. In addition, Rhode Island and Massachusetts sent men "more or less trained in the duties of signal men."

Arrangements were made so each signal station had at least one enlisted man assigned as a member of the group. On Martha's Vineyard, the site

Above: The signal corps manned an anti-artillery and aircraft warning station on Peaked Hill. Machine guns were secured by sandbags. *Courtesy of Everett Poole.*

Left: Sandbags protected machine gun nests and small buildings at the encampment on Peaked Hill. *Courtesy of Everett Poole.*

operated in Gay Head was designated as a fort. Artillery men from the Connecticut, Massachusetts and Rhode Island National Guard served as signalmen stationed at the fort in Gay Head, which was commanded by a signal corps officer from Connecticut.[70] This was the third incarnation of the signal corps on Martha's Vineyard.

Prior to World War II, Peaked Hill was used for cultivation of crops and pasturing cows, sheep, horses, oxen and swine. The site served to host summer parties and blackberry picking. (As we conducted interviews, we learned it was also used as a reasonably private place to "neck and make out." "Blackberrying" was a euphemism for making out.)

The government procured leasehold of 258.5 acres of the property in 1941 through negotiation and condemnation. The U.S. Army Signal Corps operated an Army Air Warning Service Station during the war years, from 1941 to 1947. Observers staffed Peaked Hill armed with binoculars to scan the waters, searching for German submarines. Martha's Vineyard AWS-6 was the official name of the former blackberry-picking site.

The site included generators and power lines, a motor pool, machine gun positions and a tower, all enclosed by a chain-link fence.

In 1941, tents made up the installation at Peaked Hill. Later, barracks were built for the fifty men stationed there. *Courtesy of the Martha's Vineyard Museum, gift of Susan Shea.*

On December 10, 1946, Major Kenneth A. Wood investigated and disposed of any remaining ammunition found at the "Peaked Hill Army Camp in Chilmark." Such an inspection was required in order to return the leased property under the Defense Environmental Restoration Program. Major Wood's resulting report noted more than two hundred rounds of carbine ammunition and fourteen land mine fuses were found on the site. The ammunition and fuses were delivered to the U.S. Coast Guard at Gay Head for disposal.

Bob Iadicico was at Peaked Hill following the Korean War. An experimental radar system was installed late in 1951 to verify the authenticity of objects seen with radar. MIT oversaw the project. Bob says, "I left in late 1955 for college, and I believe it was replaced by an unmanned system a year or two later [SAGE system]."

During the Cold War, from 1957 to 1970, the U.S. Air Force built a metal tower as part of the Chilmark Gap Filler Annex P-45B, a radar station.

Those walking the trails of the Land Bank Peaked Hill Reservation will come upon the site now known as Radar Hill, an enclosed area with a small building, tower and antennae. It is an updated Rescue 21.[71]

Years after World War II, in 1975, the Vineyard Open Land Foundation (VOLF) purchased half an acre of the former radar site on Peaked Hill to protect it from commercial development. VOLF, at its own expense of approximately $8,000, had the old barracks, bunker building, black-top pavement, fuel tanks and other items removed from the site.

In 1979, VOLF offered free title of the parcel to the Town of Chilmark. The town preferred to purchase a Conservation Restriction (CR) from VOLF for $15,000. That granted enforcement powers to the Chilmark Conservation Commission.

Twenty years later, Chilmark residents authorized town selectmen to acquire the radar site and assume management responsibilities for the site, in accordance with the CR. VOLF donated the site to the Town of Chilmark, declaring that this conservation property with its superb views is now in the hands of its "most appropriate steward, the Town of Chilmark."[72]

There is speculation that the U.S. Army bulldozed a few feet off the top of the site at the start of World War II, making the hill lower. Presently, if you walk the trails of the Land Bank Peaked Hill Reservation, you will find signage for both Radar Hill and Peaked Hill.

Bob Tilton recalled, "This thing came one day, and no one knew what it was. It was the first trailer truck that ever hit the island. It was a radar tower on a pair of wheels being towed by a tractor trailer truck." *Courtesy of Dave Larsen.*

The name Peaked Hill was used by the army and through history. However, according to present usage and maps, the army site was on Radar Hill; Peaked Hill is found in the Martha's Vineyard Land Bank Peaked Hill Reservation.[73]

Everett Poole remembers, "I'd go up to Peaked Hill regularly around noontime to get a free meal. There was a big mess hall. They had meat, and we here had very little, so it was a treat."

Ann Barry, a summer visitor, remembers sitting on a Chilmark stone wall early in 1942. She heard columns of marching men coming up South Road and wondered, "Where were they headed? Were they just brought over here and told to march to the west?" The men in uniform were headed to the installation atop Peaked Hill, the highest point on the island. "We teenage girls were impressed by those uniforms the men wore."

She recalled one of her favorite "duties" for thirsty military personnel: "We cousins somehow got beer and brought it to a freshwater stream at the base of the cliffs. We left it there for the men to climb down to get the cool beer we left for them." The cousins felt they were helping the soldiers by bringing them beer. "As they got their beer, it was quite exciting for us, as they wanted to visit with us as they drank their beers before bringing what was left back up those one hundred stairs to their thirsty buddies."

She went on: "One of the things about that bathing area was we didn't have to wear our bathing suits while swimming but had to put them on when we knew they were right above us. We figured that, too, was pretty cool."

At home in Chilmark on a summer evening, children played table games or listened to the radio, "to any syndicated shows along with possible war news," Barry recalled. "Looking

Bud Mayhew of Chilmark uncovered solidified sandbags, remnants of the machine gun nest at Peaked Hill. *Photo by Thomas Dresser.*

back at the radio days, I remember we all just stared at the radio as if it were a television set like today."

With little to do, local kids walked to the Chilmark Store, a common meeting place. "What I remember is that there was little, if any, traffic, and we were always barefoot." She goes on: "At the Chilmark Store, the soldiers drove down from Peaked Hill with a large tank truck for water, as there was no water at the top of Peaked Hill."

Waiting for food deliveries from down-island was a regular activity. "They might have come from SBS, which, among other things, sold groceries. I remember my aunt, in the middle of all the rationing, somehow saw to it that part of her deliveries always included a week's supply of alcohol."

"After the war, in the late summer of 1945," Barry recalls, "we were allowed access to Peaked Hill and walked up to see what was left after it was closed. One of the most striking memories was the expansive view" unimpeded by trees. She adds wistfully, "Those Chilmark days were wonderful for us kids, despite a war going on."

———

On nearby Nantucket in the summer of 1942, events brought that island closer to the war. Two boatloads of survivors from a British ship torpedoed off Bermuda arrived in Nantucket, and local Red Cross volunteers provided assistance.

And "the US Army arrived on Nantucket for the first time in history, as a company of military police took over the old Crest Hall Hotel on North Water Street. Their function in guarding Nantucket was somewhat obscure, but they were a fine body of men."[74] The soldiers remained on Nantucket until the spring of 1943.

CHAPTER 10

RATIONING

Rationing was instituted during World War II to limit consumption of items needed by the military. Early in 1942 on Martha's Vineyard, local people set up a program to ensure that minimum amounts of necessities were available for everyone, especially the impoverished, to prevent inflation and to provide the military what it needed.

A popular slogan during the war years was "use it up, wear it out, make it do, or do without." Although the independent style of thinking and improvising had been a way of life on Martha's Vineyard well before the war, islanders embraced the war effort and learned to cut corners wherever possible.

Automobile tires, which were made of natural rubber, were the first item to be rationed so military vehicles could be equipped. The Japanese controlled rubber trees on the South Pacific islands. Synthetic rubber had not yet been refined; tires were made of rubber trees. New cars came with spare tires, but owners were required to return the spares, as they were not considered essential. Recapping of punctured or older tires was in vogue.

Early in 1942, it was reported, "The setting up of tire-rationing boards on Island towns this week brings the war yet nearer to the Vineyard."[75] Tire allotment for all of Dukes County in January 1942 was eight tires for passenger cars and twenty-three tires for trucks and buses. People whined that they would revert to the days of horse and buggy or ride an ox cart, but they complied.

Oak Bluffs police chief Augustus Amaral feared thieves would steal tires; he recommended car owners record the serial number and make of tires. No reports of stolen tires were filed on-island during the war years.

Carol Carr shared a childhood memory: "I went down to the beach and found pieces of kelp, the wide, brown, squishy seaweed. I thought I could use it to make tires, as rubber rationing was underway. I brought home the slimy, brown seaweed and tried to fashion it into tires, but when it dried, it was crispy and crumpled."

Gasoline rationing followed. To obtain automobile classification based on use and need, a driver went before the local rationing board for a ration card and a book of gas ration stamps. To buy gasoline, the driver presented his classification card—A, B, C or X—along with his ration book and cash.

A card was not needed if a vehicle was an ambulance, hearse, truck, bus or taxicab. Military and government vehicles were exempt from gas rationing.

By mid-May 1942, some 1,248 automobiles were registered on the Vineyard for gas rationing. Even motorboat owners, all 92 of them, complied. Owners of tugs, ferries and fishing boats were exempt. Sightseeing and pleasure driving were restricted.

As gas rationing got underway, State Representative Joseph Sylvia assured the public there would be sufficient gas and tires for the upcoming summer season.

Freeman Leonard explained gas rationing from his perspective as one who had to drive to different Vineyard towns to screen movies, which built public morale:

I had to bring the movie down to Edgartown, a real challenge. During the war there was strict gas rationing for cars and called for a certain sticker. An A sticker meant the driver was allotted only three gallons of gas a week. B stickers went to drivers considered essential to the war effort. The C sticker, on the other hand, meant one was entitled to an almost unlimited supply of gas per week. That sticker was often assigned to a physician or minister. Fortunately, I was given the highly sought C sticker. We islanders seldom saw an X sticker, as they were assigned to members of Congress and other folks deemed very important.

How did I qualify for a C sticker? The rationing people felt my job of driving the films between towns was a necessity for wartime morale. Diversions were seen as a major benefit for those left behind to run the homes and families.[76]

His sticker read "Projectionist."

As a member of the clergy, Herman Page's father had a C sticker. Most drivers had A stickers. Gas rationing reduced visitors to the Vineyard. "We rode our bikes everywhere," Herman Page recalled. He and his father bicycled from Vineyard Haven to Edgartown for the sailing regatta. "And because of gas rationing, there were fewer cars on the road." Sailing regattas were held during the war years, as it was important to inspire young men to use their nautical skills in the navy.

After the war, Donald Mayhew learned the rationale for gas rationing: "It was not a shortage of gasoline that caused it to be rationed. Rather, rubber was the commodity in question," he explains. "The countries where most natural rubber originated were either in Japanese hands (Dutch East Indies) or required Caribbean Sea transport (Brazil). Rationing gasoline reduced the demand for tires. Even bicycle tires were rationed, and the few available were saved for delivery boys."

—————

Sugar was rationed, again, to limit cargo ships from South America. Each person had to register with the board and, oddly, to provide their complexion, height and weight.

"The total number applying for sugar rationing books on the island was 4,883 which was slightly over 88% of the island's population in 1940."[77] Each person in a household was eligible for a ration book, including babies and children; a ration book was worth six pounds of sugar.

One family in Vineyard Haven had twelve children; it was suggested they would never run out of sugar. There was some confusion over who qualified for sugar rations. Patricia Anne Rourke was born on May 4, 1942, the day sugar rationing took effect; apparently she qualified for her own ration.

Carol Carr's family ran Darling's Candy. Her father "grumbled about the government because they sent him a survey about how much sugar he was using to make the candy. My father would read it, and say, 'Ugh, I know what to do with this!'" He felt it was inappropriate for the government to ask how much sugar he needed, so he tossed the survey in the wastebasket.

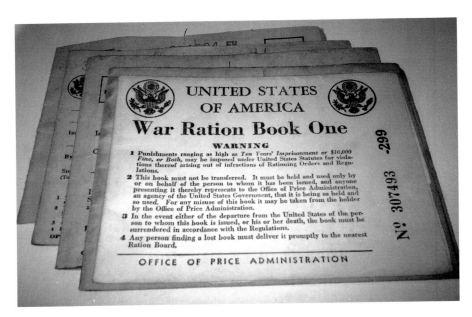

War ration books were used to limit quantity and control prices. The size of a family determined how much sugar they received. *Courtesy of Gary Soares and the Falmouth Historical Society; photo by Thomas Dresser.*

People were told to restrict coffee consumption, as it was dangerous to transport coffee beans from South America and transport ships were used to deliver munitions to the Allies. When rationed, some entrepreneurs improvised with grain, dandelions or potato peels to brew their coffee.

Betty Honey recalled, "I was working at the school in the superintendent's office. He was the director of rationing for the entire Island, and I was his secretary, and he and I made out the sugar, meat and gas and clothing rationing for the entire Island."[78] Superintendent of Schools Arthur Lord utilized his teachers to implement the program.

John Alley recalled, "My father, who was chairman of the rationing board at West Tisbury, would have to make decisions. Tires were tough." He continued: "The rationing board had to make many decisions amongst neighbors. Does a farmer take priority because he is growing things? It was an integral part of the homefront. How do we ration our resources?" He added, "If the rationing board didn't run well, then the local populace didn't do as well. Rationing boards were very important."

Some situations proved amusing. Bob Penney said, "Father was on the rationing board when food was rationed. I remember when a woman came into the Dinette [his family's restaurant] and emptied the sugar bowl into her purse; that was the end of sugar bowls on the table."

———

By 1943, additional items were rationed. Government-issued coupons were required to purchase commodities such as butter, cheese, coffee, fuel oil, lard, meat, nylon, rubber boots, shoes and silk. To prevent hoarding, ration stamps were valid for a limited time.

Rationing impacted everyone, young and old, rich and poor. It enlisted participation by the entire population in the war effort. For many, it proved the most memorable aspect of the war.

Megan Alley of Oak Bluffs has specific memories:

> We saved tinfoil from gum wrappers, cigarette packages and any other aluminum scraps and rolled them into a ball for the troops. Rationing meant you were allotted a certain number of ration stamps according to the size of a family and your job. You now had to save enough stamps to purchase butter, sugar and other items. When those items became available, you had to stand in a line to purchase them. Shoes were saved for cold weather, school and church, and most children spent the summers barefoot.

Jackie Baer recalled:

> We had to stand in line for the stamps to use them in stores such as the First National [now Midnight Farm in Vineyard Haven]. The clerks sent workers throughout the stores to fetch the customers' wants. I remember they used those "grabbers" for items on the top shelves. The clerks then added up all the items the customer ordered on a paper bag. Can you imagine someone trying to do that today? I remember George Cournoyer was so smart. He could add up on a paper bag all these long lists and never make a mistake.

In Edgartown, people shopped at Connor's Market Store on Main Street. Stella Dawley recalled, "During the week, different items became available. One didn't know what would be in the store, but we were just grateful to get what we could."

Carol Carr recalled, "I don't feel I ate any differently. Back then, you ate out of cans for vegetables, and everybody had chipped beef on toast, things like that." She remembers gas rationing. "It didn't bother us a lot because each town kept very much to itself. So we didn't go places anyway. I mean, we went to church in Vineyard Haven, but other than that, it didn't cramp our style because we walked everywhere." And the war effort overrode everything else: "You were doing it for a reason, like we saved aluminum foil and as kids we felt very patriotic about this, doing it to help."

Janet (Frye) Cunningham remembered the shortage of silk stockings: "To get the 'silk stocking look' with seams, women drew a line on the back of their legs. Nylon stockings were not generally available during the war, as any available nylon was used for making parachutes."

People complied with rationing. Peg Kelley remembered, "Mother swapped coffee coupons for sugar coupons."

And what about bananas? "Bananas had not been seen on the Vineyard for a few years. It was a great surprise that one of the markets obtained a crate or two of bananas about 1944," remembered Donald Mayhew. "They were priced at thirteen cents a pound, a very high price indeed. Still, they were sold out completely in a short time, and no bananas were seen again until the war was over."

"I remember we had a coupon book for shoes, which were rationed along with canned goods. You could stand in line at the A&P and get half a pound of butter. Butter and sugar were in short supply," Rosalie Powell recalled.

"Some of those people with a taste for sweets would give their eye teeth for sugar." Ruth Stiller recounted island intrigue: "A woman living down near Tashmoo invited my father and me down for tea on occasion, as she was so eager to make her famous cookies. She knew we would sell her a little sugar from the store [Cronig's Market] so she could make cookies. We tried not to eat too many."

One exception to rationing was meat, which was butchered by farmers who sold or gave it to neighbors, with no coupon exchange. "Living on the Vineyard meant there was lots of fish, however," Herman Page observed.

Victory gardens sprouted during the war to provide fresh vegetables, fruits and herbs; this was an effort by civilians to supplement their diet and contribute to the homefront. Small, family plots produced nearly half the vegetables grown in the United States during the war.

Vineyarders lived off homegrown food. Most people planted gardens for personal use yet offered produce to less-fortunate islanders. "Our family's victory garden took over most of our backyard," said Jackie Baer. Land behind the new Tisbury Fire Department was allotted for victory gardens. "There were about twenty garden plots back there. Each family tended their own garden." The plots were relatively small, about ten square feet. "Once the war began, some people starting raising chickens so they would always have eggs. My mother stored the eggs in a horrible substance called a 'Water Glass.' That preserved them once they were placed in a large ceramic jar in the cellar."

"Islanders never suffered from the shortage of food," said Connie Frank. "My dad had that great garden with everything you could imagine. Our family was so fortunate. We had vegetables, apples and Bartlett pears."

Metal was in short supply, as it was needed for military tanks and weapons. Aluminum, especially, was a necessity to manufacture airplanes. A new refrigerator came with one aluminum ice cube tray, not two. To buy a tube of toothpaste, the customer had to turn in an empty tube. Razor blades were limited to one per week.

"I remember at the beginning of the war my grandfather turned in his big roll of tinfoil that he'd saved for years. Big excitement," Jane Slater said.

Ruth Stiller shared a recollection: "I remember Max Miller was a junk dealer, but it wasn't 'junk' by any means. It was good solid [metal] stuff collected and sold and brought off-island for the war effort. That's how he made a living."

Rosalie Powell remembered her brother Bartlett had a wagon, "which he dragged everywhere, collecting any metal that might help the war effort. While going house to house, there was an unmistakable, loud rattle as the materials banged against each other with every road bump along the way."

"Boy Scouts collected scrap metal like old aluminum tea kettles and pans," recalled Jackie Baer. "My brother had a wagon, and he'd go up and down the streets and people gave him aluminum, which was what they really wanted. We used to save all the tinfoil and make it into balls. We took them to school where they collected them. We also saved elastic bands and string."

At the Camp Meeting office, by the Tabernacle in Oak Bluffs, one can look down for a reminder of what was once a rail track to transport luggage from the ferry. It used to encircle the Tabernacle, but the tracks were taken up during the scrap iron drive.

John Alley noted, "Several island cemeteries had old slate stones. Some creative islander figured out how to save the stones from deteriorating: they built a little roof over each stone with pieces of lead." During the war, lead was in short supply. "Most all of the cemeteries had the lead roofs removed. The local cemetery superintendent, my Uncle Fred, took all the lead off and brought it down to a collection center where they melted it into a block." Alley concluded, "All these little things added up to a huge effort. It isn't that the people were just sitting here on the island listening to the radio. They were all doing their part."

In total, 105 tons of salvaged scrap metal was shipped from Edgartown to Brooklyn, New York, on a navy barge in 1943. Funds received for the scrap were distributed among groups such as the USO, Civilian Defense, the Band and the Observation Post.

Pennies were made of steel in 1943 to reduce the use of copper. The coin was confused with a dime, however, and rusted on occasion, so it was soon discontinued.

While scrap metal could be recycled, aluminum pots and pans and old rubber tires and raincoats could not. The drives continued through the war, however, as they served as morale boosters to enlist support in the war effort.

Memorable rationing tales linger. Rationing was similar on Nantucket, recalled Jane Ray Richard. "We did a lot of little things during the war, like saving toothpaste tubes, making soap from fats and lye and mixing white oleo-margarine with orange pellets to make it look like butter."[79]

Coloring margarine was a distinct memory. Carol Carr remembered "adding coloring to oleo to make it look like butter. It had this sick orange color, but it became diluted with vegetable products."

Bud Mayhew added, "We'd get a plastic sack of margarine that was white, looked like heavy, heavy grease, and inside was a little capsule, and you'd squeeze the capsule into the grease and it would turn a deep yellow that made it look like butter."

Dairy farmers orchestrated legislation that prevented margarine from being produced already colored like butter. Margarine companies added a pellet of yellow dye for the consumer to mix into their product. With the shortage of butter, margarine sales increased.

A cartoon by Denys Wortman, courtesy of the *New York World Telegram*, was reprinted in the *Gazette*. With Wortman's memorable illustration, the caption read: "I'm saving waste paper, buying bonds, giving blood and doing what I can to get this war over. I want to see a few legs in nylons as soon as possible."[80]

"Shoes were rationed. We bought paper shoes. They were like sandals, very glamorous," recalled Betty Honey. "We would wear our paper sandals, which had high heels made of cardboard. They didn't last long, but they didn't require any kind of rationing. You could go to a dance and dance all night in them. If they got wet, that was the end of them."[81]

Patriotism was a badge of honor. Those families with sons in the armed forces were proud to acknowledge it. Service flags or banners were placed in the windows of homes with men or women on active duty in the armed forces. A blue star represented someone serving, and a gold star with a blue edge recognized someone killed in service. The gold star took precedence over a blue star and was positioned at the top of the banner.

According to Joseph Stiles, his mother was a three–blue star mother. "In those days, however many boys you got in the service, that's how many stars go in your window. All her boys were in. My middle brother was in the Army and drove a truck in the Black Ball Express in Patton's Army. My older brother was better educated and was in England and I think he had a desk job."[82]

The state guard was a program for men who did not qualify for military service due to age or physical condition. "My dad marched with the state guard, a group that replaced the national guard during peacetime," said Rosalie Powell. "The national guard was called up for federal service in the summer of 1940. My father's state guard helped maintain order, guard the coastline's important installations and was assigned to help in any emergencies or disasters."

CHAPTER 11

NURSING EFFORTS

Women served the country during the war by volunteering for the Red Cross, the United Service Organization (USO) and various Women's Corps agencies. Nursing received high prestige. Many women volunteered for the U.S. Army Nurse Corps or the U.S. Navy Nurse Corps. Teenage girls enlisted in the Cadet Nurse Corps and Junior Red Cross.

The Red Cross played a significant role in helping wounded veterans, shipping more than 300,000 tons of supplies overseas. At the military's request, the Red Cross initiated a national blood drive to collect millions of pints of blood for use by the armed forces. Mrs. Ralph Packer, chair of publicity for the Red Cross, noted in July 1943 that Katharine Cornell, of Vineyard Haven, had donated blood in the current drive in Hyannis.

A Junior Red Cross program was organized in 1940 on Martha's Vineyard, primarily to roll bandages for wounded soldiers. Quotas were set and bandages sent overseas. Rosalie Powell volunteered in the Red Cross room above the Brickman's building in Vineyard Haven: "As we entered for work, we had to put on a head piece with a Red Cross emblazoned across the front. It fastened with long, swooping ties, which ensured our hair would not contaminate the sterile dressings." Hand washing was part of the protocol.

"We were given a square template where we laid this strip of gauze, a single layer, on the template, then it had flaps that folded all four sides. You had a rhythm to follow as we folded them. You folded them and pressed on them so they'd lie flat. We made many stacks of them."

Adults recorded the hours each girl worked; this information was passed to the school department. "I received an award for the most hours worked making those dressings," recalled Powell, adding, "We had quotas in each town; the women would gather and make bandages. My aunt Lil made over ten thousand bandages and got an award from the government."

Lillian Magnuson, John Alley's aunt Lil, made over fifteen thousand bandages for the Red Cross and received awards for "homeland service to her country." "She was a driving personality on the homefront during World War II," said Alley.

Townspeople worked together. "If Edgartown wasn't meeting their quota that month," said Powell, "they banded together to use up some of their gas coupons and go for a day in Edgartown. There was someone who coordinated the get-togethers. Towns really cooperated with each other."

Early in the war, Junior Red Cross girls were "making clothing and many are knitting for European children," according to Oak Bluffs principal Charles Downs in his 1943 annual report. Money was donated to the "Crusade for Children" of the war area. The fund was "wholly for aid in war-torn Europe."[83]

Mrs. Ralph Packer promoted the Junior Red Cross, which represented justice and mercy. Vineyard Haven girls included Nancy Flanders, Ellen Packer, Mary Maciel, Dorothea Viera and Rosalie Humphreys (Powell). Oak Bluffs and Edgartown had programs as well.

Many young women participated in knitting squares for military hospitals. When the squares were completed, volunteers sewed them together as lap robes or afghans for wounded veterans.

Rosalie Powell's parents were involved in Bundles for Britain, which collected clothing for people devastated by the bombing. The office was a storefront on Main Street in Vineyard Haven, currently Cronig's Real Estate. Powell recalled, "I remember helping to sort it out and put the clothing in boxes. Then it was packed up and sent over to England."

A unique kinship arose between two communities with the same name. Powell explained, "We sent a lot of our food and fundraising efforts through our connection with Chilmark, England." A close relationship developed between people in the two Chilmarks. "My aunt Hope Flanders headed up a drive to raise money to rebuild the roof of what I believe was St. Margaret's Church in Chilmark, England." A secret English military base, which the Germans bombed, was there. "We felt very responsible for what was happening in those English towns."

CHAPTER 12

ALONG THE SHORE

Fishing was the primary economic activity for Martha's Vineyard. With the shortage of meat, fish was the staple of the Vineyard diet. "I'd go out on the fishing boats to have a good meal," recalled Everett Poole of Chilmark. "The fishermen had government checkbooks for [gas] ration stamps to supply the boats. The government wanted fish, so fishermen did pretty well during the war."

He continued: "I was running a fish market at the time, and some men came in—all dressed up—and asked for a pound of swordfish for sixty-four cents. Then they came back for another pound. They thought I must be running a front for someone since it was so profitable. They turned out to be from the OPA [Office of Price Administration]. I was fourteen years old."

———•———

During the war, the navy provided short-wave radios to fishermen to report on the presence of German submarines. Bud Mayhew recalled, "I remember my father made the antenna on his boat. You broke the seal to report a sub." Everett Poole added, "The fishermen were told to report any questionable activity. 'Well,' my father said, 'what am I going to do with this?' I don't think he ever used it. But after the war, the fishermen received commendations for using the radios."

———•———

Planes from the airfield made bombing practice runs that impacted local fishermen. Mayhew recalled, "A few fishing boats brought up a device, a depth charge or torpedo in the dragger net, because [the net] goes right along the bottom. One ship caught one in the net, pulled in the net and there was a device and the boat blew up. I think it was a depth charge." Poole added, "When the planes crashed into the ocean, the draggers would get hung up on them, and the wrecked planes would tear their fishing nets to pieces."

Vineyard youngsters combed the beaches, investigating flotsam from sunken vessels. Often, tankers left their mark.

"My grandmother had a cottage here, in Harthaven, and we spent summers there," remembered John Boardman. "When we went to the south shore, we got oil on our feet from the tankers that had been sunk by the U-boats." Bob Penney added, "Most people kept a can of gas on the deck to wash off the fuel oil from sunken tankers."

"Every Saturday morning, we would walk the beach to look for lifeboat rations," recalled Poole. "It was a big deal to find them. Once we found Hershey's Tropical Chocolate, which wouldn't melt in the sun. We also found a full case of Treet washed up on the shore. (They still sell it at the Stop & Shop.) It was like Spam. I wish I'd never dragged it home," he laughed. "The only way to eat it was to slice it really thin and fry it like bacon."

Nancy Nitchie shared a special memory: "One time, it was 1943 or 1944, we found a very attractive thing that looked like a box sewed together of canvas, with stitches going around it. We opened it up. It was surrounded with two or three enormous pieces of cork. Inside was a book from a Dutch oil tanker, with the names of everyone on the crew, over eighty people. And we found all kinds of stuff from boats being torpedoed. Life vests and oars and food sometimes would come on the beach, and gasoline drums." David Flanders found tanks of high-octane aviator gas, which his father diluted to use in his tractor.[84]

The Cape Cod Canal was especially busy during the war years. "Long convoys of merchant ships were assembled in Buzzards Bay behind anti-submarine nets and extensive mine fields as precautions because of Nazi U-boats."[85] And when the convoys gradually moved through the canal, more than one thousand feet apart, "train movements were on hold on both sides of the waterway."[86]

The cargo ship *Stephen Jones* ran aground at the northern entrance to the Cape Cod Canal on June 28, 1942. It took a month to dynamite the ship and reopen the canal. *Courtesy of the Mariners' Museum.*

In the waters off the Cape, five ships were torpedoed in the early years of the war. The German submarine *U-123* sank the tanker *Norness* off Martha's Vineyard early in 1942.

The biggest crisis in the canal occurred when the *Stephen R. Jones* ran aground at the mouth of the canal, closing the waterway. Merchant vessels were rerouted around the Cape, and one freighter was torpedoed.

CHAPTER 13

RUMORS

Before Pearl Harbor, there was talk that Martha's Vineyard would be evacuated. No reason was given except that, as an island, there was no means of protection. Civilian Defense chairman Ennis denied the story, and "his statement ended the rumor that plans were ready to be put into effect for removing people from this Island, upon the declaration of war."[87]

When it was clear the United States would enter the war, curiosity and confusion coursed through the Vineyard. But not fear. Vineyarders were confident of their safety, though stories circulated that the enemy was not so far away.

Soon after Japanese planes bombed Pearl Harbor, a rumor circulated of "hostile planes off New York city."[88] The story proved untrue, but it was accurate that the report had been planted to alert the populace. Air raid drills and citizen alerts became routine.

A story gained traction when a plane from the mainland reported that it had spotted a German submarine along South Beach. After an intense search, it turned out to be merely driftwood along the shore.

Because Martha's Vineyard was on the Atlantic shipping lanes, some people thought the island would serve as a submarine station. Rumors circulated that Tisbury Great Pond had been so designated. This story, too, had no merit.

Another story had more truth than fiction and buttressed concerns about enemy vessels offshore. A German submarine torpedoed an oil tanker, the *Combria*, off Montauk, Long Island, on January 15, 1942. All shipping, including ferry service to Martha's Vineyard, was delayed by the navy. This generated a lot of talk, much of it speculative. Nevertheless, the concern was that the submarine would attack again. The *Gazette* groused that the morning ferry did not depart until four o'clock in the afternoon, and "mails and newspapers were held up, and a funeral party bound for the Vineyard was delayed."[89]

On occasion, the *Vineyard Gazette* displayed disdain toward those from off-island. Henry Beetle Hough editorialized that the people of Martha's Vineyard must "labor under the handicap of their [press and authorities] geographical ignorance. Some high officials of the government still believe that the Vineyard is a small Island about the size of Penakese, and some think it is half way out to Bermuda."[90]

Despite the chagrin of many, the annual Agricultural Fair was cancelled in 1942. The *Gazette* fumed, "That would mean a real loss to the Vineyard, for although the fair has had to cope with difficult problems in recent years, it has represented something in Island life which is not likely to be easily replaced. This war is leaving nothing unchanged." The fair promotes local gardens and livestock and is an integral element in the community. "We should beware of breaks with the past simply because of the impatience of the present,"[91] Hough wrote.

One story captured imaginations then and now: "Those reports about the apprehension of the German saboteurs who came ashore from submarines have made thrilling reading."[92] To quell the stories, the *Gazette* lobbied for identification cards and boat permits, although the island population was so small that most people would spot a stranger.

"The latest major rumor about Martha's Vineyard, extraordinarily persistent, is to the effect that the entire Island is to be taken over by the Army, the Navy or anyway by the government."[93] While editor Hough pronounced such talk preposterous, there was more than a hint of veracity, as plans were underway to develop a satellite navy airfield on-island.

A rumor made the rounds in the spring of 1943 that soldiers from Camp Edwards had died in an explosion. "The *Gazette* learned yesterday afternoon there is definitely nothing in the story." Talk persisted for more than a week. An editorial admonished readers: "Wartime brings about exactly the right conditions for rumor to flourish."[94]

Unfortunately, two months later, the story proved devastatingly true, as four engineers of the Amphibian Brigade drowned off South Beach when their boat capsized in rough weather. When the army confirmed the tragedy, the *Gazette* proclaimed, "The rumor situation has improved greatly during the past year."[95]

In the autumn of 1943, a rumor of a plane crash from the Naval Air Facility gained traction. "Rumor is a two-edged thing," the *Gazette* editorialized. "For a long time we have been accustomed to rumors of death and disaster, but this past week false hopes have been raised again and again by stories that the six fliers from the Martha's Vineyard field have been found." Like the soldiers drowned off South Beach, the fliers from the airfield did not survive. And yet "the rumors, however, will persist without reason and without mercy, which is a great pity on all accounts."[96]

CHAPTER 14

ALIENS AND PREJUDICE

Civilian support for the war was widespread, although isolated cases of draft resistance did arise. The FBI tracked people suspected of loyalty to the Axis countries of Germany, Japan or Italy. Many people were arrested in the weeks following the attack on Pearl Harbor, and 7,000 German and Italian aliens who were not U.S. citizens were moved from the West Coast. Some 100,000 people of Japanese descent were relocated to internment camps. Enemy aliens were held without trial. United States citizens accused of supporting Germany were tried.

A case on Martha's Vineyard came to light in an interview with West Tisbury's Mike Colaneri. His father, Bert Colaneri, was a naturalized citizen, but the FBI questioned his loyalty. Bert was a longtime, well-loved Vineyard Haven barber. (His shop, once on Main Street, is now in Tisbury Marketplace.) Bert had married a local up-island woman, a sixth- or seventh-generation islander. When the war broke out, Bert was told he was not allowed to leave town, own a gun or have a radio for the duration of the war.

A local law enforcement official determined those restrictions were unnecessary. Leonard Martin, head of the state police, upon hearing the actions taken against Bert, took action on his own. He contacted the federal authorities and stated he would personally be responsible for Mr. Colaneri for the duration of the war. Concerns of the loyalty of fellow islanders were deemed unwarranted.

Donald Billings's mother was born in Venice, Italy, and became a United States citizen. When the war broke out, she had to be re-naturalized at the courthouse in Edgartown because of antagonism toward Italians.

John Boardman recalled the popular Japanese gift shop on Circuit Avenue in Oak Bluffs owned by the Sonys that sold Far Eastern trinkets, treasures and clothes. "During the 'scare,' they chased the family out of town due to the political frenzy of the time." Donald Billings remembered the war began in December, and Sony's shop was only open in the summer. Once the war began, the store never reopened in Oak Bluffs.

Joseph Stiles, born in Virginia, enlisted in the navy, trained at Quonset Point, Rhode Island, and was stationed on Martha's Vineyard in 1943 without ever having previously heard of it. On liberty, he tried to catch a bus to Boston before he learned he was on an island.

Like most African Americans, Joseph Stiles was a steward's mate with the navy, seasoning officers' dinners. "Anything that looks better will taste better," he said. He was told he would never go further than the kitchen in the navy. Unfortunately, at the time, that was true.

Joseph Stiles served in the United States Navy on Martha's Vineyard. He enjoyed life on the island and settled here after the war. *Courtesy of Joyce Stiles.*

"I was in the Quonset huts with the rest of the colored fellows and the white soldiers was in barracks, nice warm barracks, showers and everything." He did not have an easy time. "Racism on the base was so bad that many of the colored fellows were scared to go on liberty at nights; they would only go during the day."[97]

Prejudice predominated. "In the mornings, to go wash up, take showers and things, we had to walk out of the Quonset huts and go across to the nearest barracks to shower." He went on: "See, the Navy was very prejudiced. The whole armed forces was [sic] very prejudiced in those days. They recognized us as a second-class force." There was more: "The base got so bad that we couldn't eat at the same table with them when we'd go for chow; it got so bad because they had a lot of boys there that was [sic] racists."[98]

"Racism was sometimes bad on the base, but it was not anywhere else on the island," recalled Stiles. "The island people were great. That's why I came here to live, because island people always treated us beautiful. I said, 'This is the place I'm going to live in civilian life.'"[99]

Over the course of the war, prejudice within the armed forces did improve, albeit gradually, with the navy leading the way. Early in the war, First Lady Eleanor Roosevelt sought to integrate the military but met with resistance. However, in 1943, the War Department forbade discrimination in recreational facilities, a small step. And in July 1944, it ordered that military transportation must be available regardless of race. (It was another decade before the bus boycott in Birmingham, Alabama.) Aboard ship, the navy desegregated as "black and white crew members managed, with a minimum of fuss, to work, eat, and sleep together in extremely close quarters."[100] By war's end, the navy was fully integrated,[101] but it took a presidential order[102] to desegregate the rest of the armed forces.

A sense of isolation hovered over Jewish soldiers stationed on the Vineyard. "We tried to make a big effort for the Jewish servicemen because they had no place to go," said Alice Issokson. "They had absolutely no place to go, but if any of the other fellows wanted to come, it was fine. The truck would come down at certain times from Peaked Hill down to Vineyard Haven."[103]

CHAPTER 15

SERVICEMEN

Martha's Vineyard was alive with military men, from coast guard to army and navy. In Chilmark, soldiers in the signal corps came down from Peaked Hill into the village. "The men socialized by coming to the post office, which was at the Chilmark Store," recalled Jane Slater. "That was the center of town, the center of activity. The army men would come down to the post office to get their mail and hang around 'til the newspapers came in. It was a big social event." Young men from the coast guard station at Squibnocket stopped by her family's farmhouse, where her mother often baked cookies or brownies for them. It proved very popular.

The young soldiers and sailors, stationed on a remote island, were homesick. Slater recalled, "My grandmother would write letters to their parents for them. I can see her now. She wrote on big sheets of paper with purple ink. Beautiful script. And she would write these long letters to their mothers telling them how lovely it was in Chilmark." Slater smiled wistfully: "When you look back, it was a fabulous thing, and those young guys just loved it. And they called her Grammy, and they'd sit around and chat with her at night. She loved knowing what was going on. She played at being alert."

The servicemen also dropped by the Chilmark School to visit the unmarried teachers. "And as soon as they would arrive, the teachers would declare music time, and we'd all traipse into the second room of the schoolhouse and sit there and sing songs. And they loved it. And they'd laugh and sing songs with us and they had a wonderful time." Occasionally, the servicemen would drive the kids home in their Jeeps. "So we loved that. It was very exciting. We were young kids. It was great. We laughed a lot." Slater painted the experience from a teenager's perspective: "We thought of the soldiers as extended summer people. There was just the excitement of strangers. They were very youthful and a lot of fun. They would laugh."

———

At the Wayside horse farm in Chilmark, Claire Duys gave riding lessons to the servicemen. "Used to have a lot of Coast Guard boys come and ride during the war, you know, they didn't have much to do here. Used to take out a bunch of them, and they all wanted to go fast, go fast. We had all the trails in the world."[104] Claire's husband, Gerrit Duys, was Dutch and imported silk flowers and tulip bulbs from Holland.

When their son Dirk turned eighteen in 1943, he joined the U.S. Army Air Corps. He remained in the air force for thirty-three years, retiring as a colonel. Dirk's training as an aviation cadet was duly recorded in a scrapbook kept by his younger sister, Rosemarie, age eleven. Based on her brother's comments, she described the ardors of training:

"The men were classified as to whether they would become pilots, navigators or bombardiers."

"The men who were washed out or didn't pass were sent away to become either a gunner or an infantry man."

Cadets had to pass stringent mental and physical tests, with "absolutely no inside or outside ailments."

"They learned how to do loops, spins and dives and many other tricks."

"After nine weeks of hard work and good fun the men who made it were shipped off again."

Gerrit Duys, Dirk's elder brother, was deferred for medical reasons. He joined the Woods Hole Oceanographic Institute (WHOI). During the war, "there was a lot of cooperation between the boatmen at WHOI and the inexperienced landlubber scientists and technicians which made their [boatmen's] work out on the water possible."[105] This cooperative approach typified the effort to win the war.

At WHOI, "much of the research work for the Navy at this time was secret and security was much stricter than it is now. A barbed wire fence, gate, and wooden guard shack were installed on each end of the building, and everyone who worked here had to display a badge to gain entrance."[106] Security was key.

Above: Dirk Duys of Chilmark is pictured with a Piper cub. He tried to join the marines, but their recruitment office was closed, so he joined the air corps instead. *Courtesy of Terre Young.*

Right: Dirk Duys wore the air corps insignia with pride. *Courtesy of Terre Young.*

Claire Duys, Gerrit's mother, received a letter dated August 25, 1944, from the director at WHOI:

> *The work which Gerrit could do here is extremely important both to the national welfare and to Gerrit himself. Because of the confidential nature of the research work done here, it unfortunately cannot be described, but I can say unqualifiedly that as a result of it the lives of hundreds of men have been saved. The boys of Gerrit's age who are working in the Underwater Explosives Research Laboratory are more valuable to the war effort in the work they are doing in electronics than they could possibly be in the Armed Forces.*

Director Paul Cross added, "Finally, Gerrit will know he is doing his part in winning this war, and need never feel that he has failed to contribute."

Terre Young, Dirk's daughter, remembers her grandmother Claire Duys served as an air raid warden in Chilmark: "She proudly drove her car around to make certain that neighbors participated in blackout requirements" and also "housed service men assigned to the observatory

Gerrit Duys was on the crew of *Reliance*, used for explosive experiments by the Woods Hole Oceanographic Institute. *Courtesy of Terre Young.*

station on Peaked Hill. One story I remember was her dismay at not being able to help the men when they came home from practice maneuvers covered in poison ivy. None of them recognized the groundcover they were rolling around in all day."

Martha's Vineyard schoolgirls were excited to have soldiers stationed on their island. Alice Issokson recalled, "We had a good time. We had everything: we had Coast Guard; we had the Navy, the Naval base in Edgartown; we had Peaked Hill; there was always something going on. Always somebody coming and going." She went on, "And before that there had been nothing. Nothing. NOTHING."[107]

Romances budded and blossomed in the friendly atmosphere of the USO and the casual interaction between servicemen and local girls. Ann Ross recalls that her father, Bob Boren, was stationed at the coast guard station on Chappaquiddick. Her mother came from Connecticut to waitress at the Harborside. Several waitresses and coast guardsmen got together; one of the couples was Ann's mother and her father, who fell in love. Her father didn't want to return to Texas, and her mother preferred the Vineyard to Connecticut, so they settled on-island. Another coast guardsman, Billy Hannah, met his wife, Louise, on the Vineyard.

Sometimes, as Peg Kelley observed, there would be these "cute young guys leaning against the windows, watching the girls go by. Just hung around. Wasn't much for them to do."

Carol Carr worked at her family's candy shop in Oak Bluffs. "One of the things that would happen at the store was that servicemen would give me a nickel or a dime and say, 'call me after the war,' which meant call me when you grow up." As a playful comment, the phrase was harmless. Carol has a vivid memory, however, of when "two sailors came up and asked what time I got out of work, and I wouldn't tell them." She recalls that as she got out of work they were outside the store "in the shadows, watching me, by the Arcade, and so I carefully walked until I was out of sight, then I ran all the way home. And I thought, 'Mother wasn't so dumb after all!' It was very scary. It was time to beat it. I didn't like the way they were looking at me."

Megan Alley recalled her experience in Vineyard Haven: "My aunt walked us into town and would not allow us to look into the [USO] building," which afforded military men entertainment. "My grandmother told me, many years later, that my father had rescued a young woman from being assaulted when he woke to screaming and rushed outside, scaring off the attacker."

Sometimes navy men got rambunctious. It was reported that the Edgartown selectmen met with personnel from the navy airfield regarding "the problem of service men in the town in the late evening and at night." Police were told to get tough. A rowdy soldier was to be jailed at night and "then turned over to his commanding officer in the morning, which, it is believed, will soon establish a basis for satisfactory conditions."[108] In short, his supervisor would straighten him out.

The bus stop was relocated from the jail to the Edgartown Cafe (now the Wharf), "thus avoiding a necessity for the men to walk all the way through the town with opportunities and temptations for noise." Two years later, the bus route was revised again to corral rowdy sailors.[109]

A letter to the editor late in 1943 complained that "Walter L. Mayhew, driver of the Chilmark school bus, is about to discontinue driving through Tea Lane. Reason: a danger of being run down again by one of the Army trucks [from] the Takemmy encampment." The letter writer added, "Up-island here, we have found the Peaked Hill crowd and the Coast Guard, very courteous and cooperative."[110]

For several weeks in 1944, Oak Bluffs selectmen restricted servicemen from town due to "numerous complaints made about the activities of the naval men."[111] Inappropriate behavior ranged from destruction of property to preying on young girls. Lieutenant Commander Charles Webster was notified and intervened, and the ban was lifted.

In January 1945, the venerable Mansion House in Vineyard Haven banned servicemen from its fabled halls for two weeks for inappropriate behavior. "For the first time in the history of the Vineyard, so far as can be learned, and most certainly for the first time in the history of that ancient Vineyard Haven hostelry, a hotel, namely the Mansion House, has been placed out of bounds by an organization here, specifically the MVNAAF (Naval Air Field)."[112] The ban was imposed on January 19 and lifted on February 6, 1945.

In mid-summer in Chilmark, a resident complained of "a bus-load of men who bathed (in the nude) off his beach in this manner while women and children of his household were present, and who disregarded his orders

Steve Abatemarco and son Nicolas reenact the role of the World War II soldier at Camp Edwards, September 2013. *Photo by Joyce Dresser.*

Left: A World War II reenactment soldier at Camp Edwards. *Photo by Joyce Dresser.*

Right: Protective leggings worn by soldiers during World War II. *Photo by Joyce Dresser.*

to leave."[113] (The article is unclear whether it was the soldiers or family members who refused to leave.)

There were good times as well. "Did I tell you about the big Thanksgiving that we did?" asked Jane Slater, recalling a memorable event. "That was really fun," she said, warming to the seventy-year-old memory:

> *Both the coast guard and the army brought her* [my mother] *turkeys, and she cooked them in the old-fashioned kerosene stove. All through the afternoon, all the ladies in the neighborhood had cooked, and they served*

this enormous Thanksgiving dinner. And as a kid, I can remember tables set up in bedrooms. Shocking! They put the tables everywhere. My mother put linen tablecloths on every table, no matter what it was, and then my brother and I—and probably other kids, I don't remember—our job was to circulate biscuits and rolls. We went around. It was so much fun. They would come in, find an empty spot, get a plate of food, they'd leave and the next batch would come in. It was all afternoon. When they were free, they'd come in. And it really was a production, it just happened.

CHAPTER 16

UNITED SERVICE ORGANIZATION

The United Service Organization (USO) was an effort whereby local communities provided entertainment and information to troops stationed far from home. Very early in the war, Mrs. Jane Hope Whitney, head of the Falmouth USO, visited soldiers stationed at Peaked Hill. "She was pleased to know that the uniform is equivalent to a ticket of admission to many Island affairs, as has not always proved to be the case on the mainland."[114] Martha's Vineyard women planned to organize a local USO chapter.

By April 1942, a branch of the USO had opened on Main Street Vineyard Haven. A fundraiser at the Tisbury School, featuring skits by Peaked Hill soldiers, drew more than seven hundred people.

The USO became an island entity. The *Gazette* commented, "Mrs. Jane Whitney was here on Wednesday as usual, and the usual programs of music and films was [*sic*] held at the Vineyard Haven club room." The newspaper explained the role of the USO: "Speaking generally, the USO looks after the enlisted man when he is off duty, and the Red Cross looks after him when he is on duty."[115]

Hector Asselin recalled they had table tennis at the USO. "And my future wife, they couldn't beat her." Eva Allen was a local girl whom Hector met at the USO. He smiled at the memory of more than seventy years. "They had special dinners and dances," he added. On occasion, he would screen movies at the USO.

Oak Bluffs soon had a USO room as well. "The bus stop was at the alley by Secret Garden, which was a hot dog stand," recalled Donald Billings.

"There was a USO center on Main Street in Vineyard Haven," recalled Megan Alley. It was across from the current Santander Bank. *Courtesy of Chris Baer.*

"Soldiers would get a hot dog or stop at the drugstore before going back to the base." Later, the USO was next to the Strand Theatre as "an info center and rec room, with books, magazines, writing materials and sewing kits. A telephone has been installed."[116]

Clara Marshall, an island girl, recalls that her father, John Frank Bush, from Alabama, was in the navy, stationed at the naval airfield. "He worked as a mechanic on the airplanes," Marshall said. "He met my mother, Elizabeth Ann DeMello, at the USO, where they would listen to music and dance." Another USO connection.

Katharine Cornell headlined a USO fundraiser[117] at the Tisbury School in August 1942. "Of course Miss Cornell will be right there, the Martha's Vineyard Miss Cornell, and it is noised about [*sic*] that she may sing a song, which is something she has not yet done on the stage." The auditorium was jammed; soldiers served as ushers. The evening opened with Guthrie McClintic, Miss Cornell's husband, and featured Nancy Hamilton, Bob Hawk and Gregory Peck. Kit Cornell's Jamboree raised over $1,500 for the USO, and yes, she did sing on stage.[118]

Jane Slater remembered that her mother was a senior hostess at the USO on Wednesdays. "She'd take the Chilmark girls in our Model A Ford, and any servicemen that needed a ride, and go down to the dance." Romances blossomed: "Over the course of the couple of years she did it, she fostered two marriages: Marshall Carroll, a soldier up at Peaked Hill, and Bette Flanders, a local girl. And Bill Seward of the coast guard, stationed up at Squibnocket, and Barbara Flanders, another local girl, got married."

Donald Billings recalled the USO room in Oak Bluffs on Circuit Avenue, in the building that now houses Craft Works and Sanctuary. *Courtesy of Chris Baer.*

Bette (Flanders) Carroll recalled, "I was knitting squares with another woman in town, and she said, 'Why not come down to the hall tonight [USO in Vineyard Haven]. Some other women will be there.' So I went along, and he [Marshall Carroll, aka 'Curly'] came in there. I guess he took a shine to me. And he must have liked me because we were together for a lot of years."

Curly Carroll was stationed at Peaked Hill, a member of the signal corps. Bette told her story: "We went to Florida. I told him his family saw things differently from me. His family asked if I liked squash, and I said I did, but they served squash with onions, and I said, 'I'm going home. And are you coming with me?' and he did." She added, "He loved it when he came here. He went fishing; he had a boat. He really liked it here."

The USO linked local residents with servicemen stationed on Martha's Vineyard. Newspaper reports mentioned dances and dinners in the down-island communities of Vineyard Haven, Oak Bluffs and Edgartown. The Vineyard Haven USO celebrated its first anniversary in 1943, and an open house at the Edgartown USO utilized a ping-pong table to serve tea. USO girls, from teenagers to housewives, socialized with the soldiers.

"A lot of us girls hung out at the USO during the war," recalled Ruth Stiller. "We had the best time of our lives because we were so outnumbered. We had dances, and of course, you were asked to dance all the time. We would go as often as we could. The guys from the base would come, and we were invited every night if we wanted to go."[119]

———

An influx of the Engineer Amphibian Brigade from Camp Edwards occurred when soldiers landed in Edgartown and roamed the streets, seeking entertainment. More than five hundred men were fed at the Edgartown USO and wandered from the drugstore to the barbershop to the home of Emily Post. Townspeople took this intrusion in stride.

Bob Tilton, as a young teenager, proudly worked at the Vineyard Haven USO. Each day, he raised the American flag, doing his part for the war effort.

The USO continued to offer services to the servicemen. In the spring of 1944, it was reported the USO rooms in Oak Bluffs, Vineyard Haven and Edgartown had recorded more than six thousand visits. That summer, the *Gazette* noted, "The Island has been unfailing in providing USO services for the men assigned here, most often, of course, complete strangers."[120] And that is what made the program such a welcome entity in the community.

"They had a Wurlitzer. It played records. Like a jukebox." Hector Asselin recalled the iPod of the 1940s. "You had choices of whatever you wanted to play. Record drops down and plays." *Courtesy of Chris Baer.*

CHAPTER 17

THE VAN RYPER MODEL SHOP

The homefront on Martha's Vineyard wore many faces, none more intriguing than the Van Ryper Model Shop in Vineyard Haven. The company made model ships and airplanes, called recognition models, used by the navy during the war.

Freeman Leonard worked for Charles Van Ryper:

> *Charles Van Ryper, my boss, was an interesting man. In the early 1930's, while living in Maine, he started making ship models. People really liked them and commissioned him to make models of actual vessels they'd once been on. They provided photos of liners, freighters and even some private yachts. From them, he created miniature models. A hobby flourished into an unexpected business.* [121]

Charles Van Ryper moved his operation to Martha's Vineyard, a haven for sailing ships, in 1933. The shop began with a single building by the current Seaworthy Gallery on Beach Road, Vineyard Haven, with a staff of eight.

Van Ryper's reputation grew; his models of past and present ships were constructed with painstaking detail, perfectly scaled. He specialized in island steamers and transatlantic liners; orders came from shipping firms, naval architects and steamship lines.

A model airplane by Van Ryper. Aircraft were designed to be photographed "in flight" to create illustrations for aircraft-recognition pamphlets. *Courtesy of Bow Van Ryper.*

The Van Ryper story is best told by Bow Van Ryper, who shared recollections of his grandfather: "The first war-related contract came in 1940, from the Maritime Commission, which wanted a large-scale model of an EC2-S-C1 freighter, the vessel that, mass produced by the thousands, would become the famous Liberty Ship."

And then:

An order from the Navy Department followed in mid-1941: one hundred sets of twenty-three Japanese warship models apiece, built to the navy-standard 1:500 scale. They had fewer small details (masts, funnels, railing) than the shop's standard merchant-ship models and were painted a uniform flat, dark gray color overall (presumably to navy specifications). The "recognition models" (as they were known) ended at the waterline and were screwed onto narrow strips of blue-painted quarter-inch plywood.

These models were training aids to familiarize sailors and airmen with the silhouettes of enemy vessels. *Courtesy of Bow Van Ryper.*

A box akin to a wooden briefcase protected each model for transport.

Van Ryper continued: "The 2,300 Japanese-fleet recognition models were completed and delivered to the navy before Pearl Harbor and evidently met with the service's approval. Further orders for similar sets of German and Italian vessels followed in early to mid-1942."

———

The Van Ryper model shop ventured into airplane models as well, according to Van Ryper:

> *The shop's woodworking facilities also turned out a series of scale models of German and Japanese aircraft. Japanese aircraft (fighters, medium bombers, floatplanes and flying boats) predominated, but the navy also ordered models of German Ju-87 "Stuka" dive bombers, Ju-88 medium/ dive bombers and FW-200 long-range patrol planes, all types used by the Luftwaffe for anti-shipping attacks in the Mediterranean and North Sea during the early years of the war.*

———

Leonard said:

> *We made a submarine that was eight inches long and painted it a natural color. Then we made one half that length, and painted it a darker color. Then we made one half that—so now you're down to a two-inch model that had to have the exact same silhouette as the eight-inch model. And we had to make twenty models of each.*[122]

Aviators used the model ships to identify silhouettes and deck plans of enemy ships. The models had to be accurate up close, as well as from a distance.

"Our fame grew," said Freeman Leonard. "But so did demands." He added, "To ensure quality, the government sent Naval inspectors to our shop to inspect our work before they paid us. No problem. We did good work."

He added, "I wasn't an active participant in the combat missions, but felt I contributed to the war effort through those models."

Models were made of poplar, with lacquer finish. Sheets of clear plastic, heated and shaped, mimicked aircraft Plexiglas canopies and nosecones. Van Ryper was known for attention to detail and unlimited variety of ships and planes. *Courtesy of Bow Van Ryper.*

As orders from the navy poured in, the Van Ryper shop expanded from one building to three and employed up to fifty men and women working two shifts. And there was more, said Bow Van Ryper:

The shop's other major contribution to the war effort was the production of highly detailed, large-scale models of specific vessels—merchantmen and warships alike—for display in the offices of shipyards, shipping lines and possibly also naval installations. The navy produced small-scale models of American warships in house in their own model-making shops. At least one large Van Ryper model—of a Liberty Ship—wound up in the collection of President Franklin D. Roosevelt.

A singular Van Ryper model based on actual blueprints was nearly thirty feet long. It was a model of the T-2 tanker, specifically made for the Kaiser shipyard in Oregon, which manufactured the full-size tanker. This model showed shipbuilders how to actually construct the vessel.

Bow Van Ryper explained: "It was constructed entirely of metal (by a team of workers led by the shop's chief metalsmith, Stanton H. 'Hun' Lair) and duplicated not the ship's exterior hull plating but its interior structure."

In July 1942, a fire, ostensibly caused by an overheated light bulb, incinerated much of the Van Ryper factory. Damage approached $25,000.[123] The fire "gutted the shop—destroying the plans as well as the unfinished fifth section of the model (the first four had already been shipped west)— and a replacement set of blueprints was flown in from Oregon so work could continue."

The *Vineyard Gazette* recognized the import of the Van Ryper shop: "Making builders' scale models for the American shipping program, the Van Ryper establishment became a genuine war industry."[124]

Van Ryper employees enjoyed their work. Charles Van Ryper gathered workers around Stan Lair's living room piano once a week to make music. Workers played clarinet, trumpet, piano and sax in the jam sessions.

Jackie Baer remembered, "My father, Stan 'Hun' Lair, was an air raid warden. At thirty-nine, he was too old for the draft. He gave up his plumbing business in Vineyard Haven and went to work for Van Rypers, making ship models that were used for military purposes."

"The Van Rypers were wonderful people," recalled Ruth Stiller. "They usually didn't hire young people, not in my age group. Most were in the low twenties. They made beautiful ship models."

———

The Van Ryper model shop contributed to the war effort far beyond the confines of Martha's Vineyard. By late 1943, however, the navy had met its need for recognition models, the shop slowed down and reverted to its original purpose: building individual model ships.

———

A peculiar memory remained with Leonard:

> *One day, a naval officer walked into our shop in full uniform adorned with all kinds of braid, ribbons and awards. I couldn't help but notice his various awards and had to comment: "For a little shop like this you're wearing an awful lot of stuff."*
>
> *He replied, "Young man, I'm second in the country. When you get this job, and you're going to get it, you'll know why I was here."*
>
> *He started asking about our work and wanted to see samples. He had come with a secret order to turn out a new batch of boats and bombers, in case the war took a terrible and unexpected turn. They had hired us to make boats and bombers, which belonged to the Soviet Union! The Russians were our allies but our navy still wanted models made of any potential enemy's ships.*[125]

CHAPTER 18

FERRYBOATS *NAUSHON* AND *NEW BEDFORD*

To defeat the Axis powers, the Allies had to stage a landing on the continent. Initially, plans were made to invade Europe in the autumn of 1942 but were delayed as the Allies, especially Churchill, realized they were not yet ready for such an invasion. Instead, troops invaded North Africa to land from the sea, bomb from the air and move inland. This North African invasion, through the winter of 1942–43, proved a trial run for the Normandy invasion in June 1944.

The Allies required troop transport ships to cross the English Channel. An unfortunate but necessary element of an invasion was the need for hospital ships for the wounded. The navy faced a critical shortage, as navy vessels were already involved in combat; there was neither time nor means to build hospital ships.

A British captain proposed use of American ferryboats. "The behavior of such craft on the ocean, even in fair weather, was problematical; and an Atlantic gale could prove disastrous. Accordingly, careful preparations were made."[126]

Two pleasure steamboats, the *Naushon* and the *New Bedford*, were steady, sturdy ferries of the New Bedford, Martha's Vineyard and Nantucket Steamboat Company. The navy appropriated these two vessels in the summer of 1942.

"The *Naushon*, pride of the Island fleet of steamers, yesterday took her last look at the Island, which she has served since she was built in 1929," the *Gazette* wrote reverently. "She has been taken over by the federal

The *Naushon* steamed from New Bedford to Martha's Vineyard for a dozen years before it joined the Honeymoon Fleet in 1942, the flotilla of ferries that headed off to Europe. *Courtesy of the Mariners' Museum.*

government and will play her part in the war effort, in some capacity not divulged." An editorial spoke to the need for "auxiliary craft of service and supply" but did not speculate what or where. "She will serve the nation as she served these Islands, and nothing that floats can make a prouder record."[127] The *Naushon* was the flagship of the steamship company, some 250 feet long and 60 feet wide, capable of accommodating 2,030 passengers. Its engine had been converted from coal to oil.

Less than a month later, the navy sought a second ferry, the *New Bedford*, from the same steamship line. The obvious result felt by residents of the Vineyard was a reduction in ferry service, down to two trips per day.

While the navy used the war power of the government in taking the two ferries, a *Gazette* editorial argued that "the Vineyard and Nantucket have done just about all that is possible. Both island communities are doing their utmost to support the war effort."[128]

In the later summer of 1942, eleven ferryboats were assembled in Philadelphia to be strengthened for the arduous Atlantic crossing and refitted as hospital ships. The outer staterooms of the *Naushon* were converted to nurses' quarters. The promenade deck became a wardroom for officers. Bunks for wounded soldiers were installed on what had served as the freight deck for sixty automobiles; the area was petitioned into wards.

The *Naushon* "was camouflaged and boarded up. After her arrival here she was painted white with a green stripe running fore and aft just below the boat deck and with several large crosses on her sides and stack."[129] Furthermore, "the vessels had their open spaces boarded up and a heavy 'turtle-back' built across the foredecks to ward off heavy seas."[130]

While undergoing renovations, two of the eleven steamers were deemed structurally unsound, and a third burned to the waterline.

This fragile fleet, made up of eight converted steamboats and escorted by a pair of British destroyers, departed St. John, Newfoundland, on September 21, 1942. "The convoy, designated RB-1 [the RB denoted 'riverboat'], headed out to sea at a speed of 15 knots and set a course for Iceland where the ships were to refuel."[131] The flotilla was nicknamed the Honeymoon Fleet for the optimistic opportunity it was designed to provide to the war effort.

Second Officer Raymond Brewer commented on the *Naushon*: "She might be an old ferry boat, but she took the Atlantic like the *Queen Mary*."[132]

The first few days were uneventful, "but an Admiralty radio message brought word that enemy submarines were known to be active in the area." The crisis intensified. "Noon chow was nearly completed when a fiery explosion suddenly engulfed the flagship *Boston*! Two German torpedoes streaking across the blue sea had shattered her hull and broken her back!"[133] The crew was rescued by the *New Bedford*. The *New York* was also torpedoed. A third steamer, the *Yorktown*, was sunk on the sixth day.

"The *Naushon*, commanded by Captain J.J. Murray, a genial Irishman from Waterford, did not use her guns, but took successful evasive action by bold alterations of course and steaming to maximum speed." All day the *Naushon* evaded U-boats, "with escorting destroyers and convoy supporting each other grimly."[134] Of the *Naushon* and *New Bedford*, it was written: "Since they were of very shallow draft, torpedoes aimed at them apparently went underneath their hulls and neither was harmed."[135]

The steamship *New Bedford* also plied the waters off Martha's Vineyard. It was converted to a troop transport ship after the war. *Courtesy of the Mariners' Museum.*

The remaining five ferryboats made it to port in Ireland and England. King George honored the officers of the steamers.

The *Naushon* became hospital ship number 49, stationed in London, part of the British navy with a British crew. It was staffed by American doctors, nurses and three young Red Cross women, who bunked in the bow.

A military publication made light of the dramatic crossing and then celebrated the *Naushon*:

> *The prodigal ferry boat, who, weary of wending her way between New Bedford and Martha's Vineyard while her big sisters were sailing the bounding main, tooted a final goodbye to the man who played the concertina on the upper deckerina, joined the Navy and several days later arrived in London.*[136]

CHAPTER 19

SHIPBUILDING

The Edgartown sloop *Priscilla V*, owned by Captain Jared Vincent, was appropriated by the U.S. Navy Department in the spring of 1942. "This was the first taking of an Island craft for conversion to war purposes."[137] The *Priscilla V* was to be used as a boarding/freighting vessel by the navy. (Captain Vincent was handed a receipt but had no idea if he would be reimbursed. He did eventually receive compensation and built a new fishing boat larger than the *Priscilla V*.)

The Martha's Vineyard Shipbuilding Company, owned by William Colby,[138] was awarded a contract by the navy to build ships. This was the first time warships were built on Martha's Vineyard. Island men, money and material were devoted to the war, and Colby's was congratulated for contributing to the war effort. The company sought twenty men experienced in building boats.

Teenager Herman Page worked at Colby's. "They had a contract to build barges," he recalled. "They were wooden, open and used to carry coal, among other things. The yacht business was down during the war, so the shipyard needed contracts for other boat building. I was seventeen or eighteen, and I would hold the boards until they were nailed in place. I was employed for six or seven weeks. And I got a lot of blisters! They were heavy beams."

He added, "The barges were built in an open area of the beach" by the motel and gas station.

Connie Frank recalled, "Barges were being built right where DeSorcy's is now, in the Vineyard Haven Harbor. These were contracted by the navy and got started right after the war started." Bud Mayhew added, "Martha's Vineyard Shipyard, Colby's, was building barges during the war for the landing in Normandy. Built them on the beach and slid them, sideways, down a ramp into the water. The Art Cliff was a trolley car to feed the workers."

The shipyard produced three kinds of boats, according to Arthur Railton: "honey" barges to haul garbage, small landing craft to ferry marines ashore and boats to haul bombs and depth charges to navy seaplanes at their moorings. Bob Kinnecom, interviewed in 1999, said, "I worked at the shipyard at this time, just before going into the service, and used to deliver these boats to New Bedford. They were known as 'Plane Re-Arming Boats' and were employed to carry armaments out to large seaplanes anchored offshore."[139]

Work on the first vessel for the navy progressed through the autumn of 1942; it was launched after the new year. Wartime censorship curtailed specifics about the vessel. A newspaper article read, "Someday, when world conditions are different, the *Gazette* will be able to publish all details connected with this undertaking, which has interested the entire Island, and many mainland points as well."[140]

This navy tender serviced seaplanes moored in the harbor. It had a protective rubber bumper. The tender was built by the Martha's Vineyard Shipyard. (Shipyard files were searched for images, but wartime censorship limited photographs.) *Courtesy of Chris Baer.*

The article continued: "All that can be said now, however, is that the boat-builder and the house-carpenter, working with their own gangs and a few specialists, went to work on ship construction, and turned out a job that the War Department has viewed with satisfaction and pleasure."[141]

Two months later, the launch of another navy ship at Colby's was delayed slightly. "An unsuitable mixture of grease on the ways (skids) caused the craft to stick just before she entered the water."[142] The tide had fallen, so the launch was postponed until high water the next day.

By the summer of 1943, headlines proclaimed a booming industry: "Boat Building Looms Large in War Effort." A rare *Gazette* photograph shows the bow of a vessel being christened by Mrs. Stephen C. Luce Jr., wife of the Civilian Defense director.[143]

Artist, author and illustrator Melvern Barker (1907–1989) painted four murals in William Colby's office between 1942 and 1944. The scenes depict construction of boats requested by the navy during the war. The boats were scows that picked up rubbish from navy vessels, plywood launches to transport marines and tenders that took bombs and depth charges to amphibian patrol planes (seaplanes). The murals were donated to the Town of Tisbury in 1986 by Tom and Phil Hale of the Martha's Vineyard Shipyard and are hung in the lower level of the Tisbury School, the only school building still extant from World War II.

At the height of its work for the navy, the Martha's Vineyard Shipbuilding Company employed eighty-five men, local boat builders and carpenters. The yard built, fitted, launched and delivered nearly one hundred ships for the army and navy. Most were small boats, but "it speaks well for the enterprise of William A. Colby and his partner, William E. Dugan, that such a small outfit, with no previous record of the kind, should have been able to operate so successfully."[144]

CHAPTER 20

THE INVASIONS OF MARTHA'S VINEYARD

Among the more unusual wartime episodes on Martha's Vineyard was the series of practice invasions in the late summer of 1942.

The remote location of Martha's Vineyard presented an opportunity for mock invasions. Although war games were deadly serious, there was an aura of humanity in reporting what took place. George Hough recorded intriguing details in his wartime diary: "Three jeeps at Fish Hook at noon. Escorted them to the Allen House. Herbert [Norton] told us troops were encamped on the road to the Christiantown chapel." Hough was in the midst of army activities: "To the Nortons where I had a message from Camp Edwards from Major Christie. Found the Allen house converted into an Army barracks, but no one there. Posted message on main entrance." Hough portrayed himself as intimately involved in this military exercise.

Amid all the excitement, he captured the moment with an aside: "My trusty Captain Cottle and his runner-up young Fisher, asked permission to postpone mowing the lawn until the war is over." (Captain Eddie Cottle was from Cottle's Lumber on Lambert's Cove Road.)

Hough offered assistance to the invading forces: "A little later on a detachment of soldiers—the invaders—came up to the house and I guided them over to Indian Hill. Later arrived the jeep with two lieutenants asking the way to Gray's Beach [on the north shore]. Rode over to my boundary line with them." Hough was as much a part of the operation as possible.

Meanwhile, neighbors gathered at the highest point on Indian Hill, Mary Guerin's house, to survey military maneuvers unfolding below at

Left: Dark lines indicate transport vessels ferrying troops across Nantucket Sound for the practice invasion of Martha's Vineyard in the autumn of 1942. *Courtesy of the National Archives; photo by Thomas Dresser.*

Right: John Hough is the great-grandson of George Hough, whose logbook recounted the 1942 invasion. *Photo by Thomas Dresser.*

Lambert's Cove, where troops had landed. At dinner that night, Hough's story continued:

> *Virginia Berrisford (artist) came down for supper bringing a baked casserole of jambayla of her own composition. Superb! Three soldiers turned up as we were eating supper and asked for water. "Would you rather have a beer?" I asked. They preferred beer and consumed two quarts. Open house for the Army officials. Jolly hour with them until Virginia had to leave before darkness in blackout Chilmark. The boys lingered and started for camp in the dark.*

Previously, back at the *Gazette*, Henry Beetle Hough had editorialized about the impending invasion: "The soldiers are coming to Martha's Vineyard— our own soldiers on maneuvers which are part of their training for that decisive part of the great war which lies ahead." He was prescient in his observations. "When they land along the north shore and make their way up through the woods and rocky hills, and the news of their arrival spreads, the chances are that most inhabitants of Martha's Vineyard will think of another landing to be made in the future, on some enemy coast beyond remote waters."[145]

These maneuvers were indeed training for the invasion of North Africa late in 1942 and manifest again, most importantly, in the invasion of Normandy, D-Day, on June 6, 1944.

And yet, when troops did land on Martha's Vineyard in August 1942, there was not a word in the *Gazette*. Censors strictly curtailed the press from reporting on the maneuvers.

On Indian Hill, war maneuvers continued the next day, August 20, as George Hough was awakened by the sound of a large military vehicle whose driver was lost. Hough directed him to his destination and then dealt with a pressing landlord dilemma: "Went to the Allen house to express my sorrow to the General [Keating] whom I poisoned [*sic*]. He was taken violently ill Tuesday night and attributed his illness to the water and asked to have it boiled." Without hesitation, Hough responded: "Apon boiled it smelled like sulphur hydrogen. Investigation revealed a dead rabbit and two dead rats in the Allen house reservoir." George Hough had his well cleaned, and "all the officers joined in praise of the Nortons and the Allen house accommodations."

The invasion concluded that evening: "The roar of diesel engines continues as troops are being embarked in barges. The war ended tacticly [*sic*] at 10 o'clock."

While restricted from publishing reports on the invasion, the *Vineyard Gazette* did print a front-page letter on August 25, 1942, that read, in part: "I want to extend our sincere appreciation and thanks for the many courtesies which the inhabitants of Martha's Vineyard have shown us. I have not heretofore seen a group of citizens so genuinely sincere in their friendliness as those on your little Island." It was signed by Brigadier General Frank Keating of the HQ Amphibious Training Command, Camp Edwards. Keating had bunked at the Allen house and suffered ill effects of the polluted well water yet appreciated Vineyard hospitality. He had been promoted to brigadier general during the maneuvers.

———

While the Houghs, father and son, viewed the mock invasion through reporters' eyes, the army considered it a serious training exercise. The Amphibious Training Center analyzed the maneuvers:

> *The training of the 45th Infantry Division (Texas National Guard) was terminated with a three-day amphibious exercise. The exercise involved a tactical situation concerned with the assumed occupation by German forces of Martha's Vineyard, an island in Vineyard Sound off the south shores of Cape Cod. The task of the division was to invade the island, drive out the German forces and secure the island with its airfield as a base for further operations against German forces occupying Nantucket Island.*[146]

The Forty-fifth Division was composed primarily of the federalized Texas National Guard. The exercise was intended to be as realistic as possible in the limited area. "Demolitions were planted on the beaches and inland to be exploded during the landing to simulate naval gunfire support, artillery fire, and land mines."[147]

The Vineyard was defended by the Seventy-fifth Composite Infantry Training Battalion, "but the number of troops available in that unit was small, which resulted in the use of flags and umpires to represent the enemy on a part of the island."[148]

Parachutists dropped over the (Katama) airfield. Troops stormed the beaches. Observers evaluated the exercise, commenting that troops had to be halted too soon, which "tended to make them lose interest in the problem."[149]

"Despite the numerous handicaps," Captain Becker's report continued, "the exercise was carried out successfully on 18, 19 and 20 August, amid loud explosions, smoke screens, dropping parachutists, and the roar of landing craft motors." In assessing the invasion, "the lessons learned from the execution of the maneuver did not reflect unfavorably upon the Amphibious Training Center."

The report concluded, "The majority of the unfavorable comments of observers were directed toward irregularities caused by violation of basic

LCM (landing craft, mechanized), bow raised. These boats, developed by Andrew Jackson Higgins of New Orleans, were invaluable in speedy, safe troop landings. *Courtesy of the National Archives; photo by Thomas Dresser.*

training principles on the part of individuals, such things as using lights and smoking in the open at night, bunching of individuals, poor road discipline, improper camouflage."[150]

The Engineer Amphibious Brigade failed to land troops at specified times on designated beaches. New procedures were implemented in the brigade, including boat operation, navigation, shore-to-shore operations, supply distribution and signal communications. Night operations, with compasses and maps, as well as mine-removal techniques, were studied. And the means to safely and swiftly transport troops onto beaches was revised.

Riley Deeble described challenges that faced the Allies in an invasion:

> *The Allies had been working on the technology of landing on the beach, all the way back to World War I, in the Dardennelles and the Mediterranean at Constantinople. They attempted to land on an open beach under the face of fire, and it didn't work very well. When troops landed on the beach, you had the standard navy rowboat. The guys would row right up to the beach. The guys just couldn't do it.*

Andrew Jackson Higgins was a great boat builder in New Orleans. The coast guard requested fast, little boats. When the Allies contemplated the idea getting troops ashore in the face of the Nazis, they said, "Let's figure a way to land on the beaches instead of the ports." This was solved when you saw the Normandy beaches.

Getting boats specially developed for that was the goal. The Higgins boats did not have the conventional rounded bow. They shaped the bottom of the boat so it would go up on the beach better. The bow had a ramp that went down, then people could walk off and tanks and trucks could drive off.

To land soldiers on beaches under enemy fire, the army utilized the small, speedy boats developed by Andrew Jackson Higgins. Men of the Engineer Amphibious Command (EAC) piloted the landing craft to bring troops ashore.

The EAC was created on June 10, 1942 by the War Department, specifically "for the purpose of organizing and training Army personnel in the operation of landing craft and the establishment of beach heads."[151] The EAC operated the LSTs (landing ship, transports) and LCMs (landing craft, mechanized). At Camp Edwards, men were trained to maneuver the boats onto beachheads so tanks, trucks or personnel could disembark.

Riley Deeble was a member of the amphibious brigade. He learned to pilot an LCM across Vineyard Sound and was knowledgeable in invasion training techniques. He recalled:

I was in Company C, the boat regiment, and we were stationed at Cotuit (Can Do It). Almost every day we'd get in the landing craft and take the boat over to East Beach on Chappaquiddick. That's where I learned to operate the LCM; that was the largest landing craft. [An] LCM could carry one tank, or one 6x6 truck or one hundred men. I operated it with a crew of two.

We would cross from Cotuit to East Beach. On the LCM, the ramp covered the whole bow. You'd push it up on the shore. That was fantastic. No great trick. Get it ashore, then drive it in, the bow would be easy. There was a lever to open the ramp.

To land the men on the beach was key to success. Troops would dash across the sand and make cover in bushes along the shore. Proper placement of the landing craft on the shore was the first element.

LCM, bow down. These vessels transported men and machines in practice invasions of Martha's Vineyard. They were integral to the North African campaign and later on the beaches of Normandy. *Courtesy of the National Archives; photo by Thomas Dresser.*

Once troops disembarked, "backing out was very difficult," Deeble continued, "because all the weight, the engines, was in the stern, and that was, of course, pivotal." Larger boats could ease off the beach, but "we had to concentrate to learn to back; we didn't have a cable to rely on."

"I landed on Chappy to learn how to do it, must have been about twenty times. I remember my sergeant shaking his head, saying, 'You're never going to get it!' Actually, I did! And I was promoted to technician, third grade."

John Daggett, who lived on the Vineyard north shore, recalled seeing landing craft that "would come directly to the beaches, let down the wide ramp that formed a part of their snub-nosed bow, and out would come many men with their guns. They would have practice landing on and securing the beach. Often some of the men got lost and the fleet returned without them. We provided food and shelter until a boat was sent for them."[152]

Troops gained experience in water landings, tidal flow and the means to unload personnel. When the army felt comfortable in use of these landing craft, the flotilla of military vessels paraded down Vineyard Sound.

Francis Fisher, ninety-seven and a very unassuming man, was the second man from Edgartown to enlist in World War II. He was among the five thousand soldiers who boarded LSTs to cross Vineyard Sound in the mock invasions of 1942. Fisher recalls that his LST landed by Bend-in-the-Road Beach, at Cow Bay. The men disembarked and tramped across the Edgartown Golf Club, kicking up the sod, then rode by truck down to Katama, where they put up tents. As a cook, Fisher was responsible for feeding many of the troops.

Francis Fisher was not permitted to visit his family, right there in Edgartown, as he was on a military mission. As one of the few Vineyarders participating in the invasion, he knew his way around and was aware the locals disapproved of those servicemen who were unruly or disruptive.

Fisher took part in the Normandy invasion and then moved on to Belgium by the German border. He called the fighting "terrible," with many men injured or killed by shrapnel. "I was some lucky," he recalls. After the war, true to his name, he became a shell fisherman.

A second invasion of Martha's Vineyard was planned for October 1942. With additional training and education, the Amphibious Training Center believed its troops, which now included the federalized Thirty-sixth Division of the Texas and Oklahoma National Guard, were ready for practice combat.

"It was planned that on this proposed D-Day [October 2, 1942] at H-hour [dawn] the main attacking force would land on Red Beach [Lambert's Cove] while supporting units landed on nearby Yellow and Green Beaches."[153]

John Galluzzo described the invasion: "October 2–3, 1942, the 1st and 2nd Engineer Amphibian Brigades prepared for a classified training exercise, the invasion of Martha's Vineyard. The 36th Infantry Division was the force that was to liberate the Vineyard from the 'enemy.'" Supplemented by a map of troop movements, the account continued: "The troops got in their boats with their equipment the night before the training. They hit the beach at first light. As they approached the shore, they came out of the night in silence, right on time."[154]

The main invasion occurred an hour and a half before daybreak. "Across the dripping and chilly waters of Vineyard Sound moved the first wave of amphibious infantrymen being ferried by the amphibian engineers."[155]

Another account of the invasion was written years later by Anthony Cimino, who served as commander of Camp Edwards in the 1980s:

The First Engineer Amphibian Brigade ended its training with an invasion of Martha's Vineyard. The 36th Division was the combat unit. Troops and equipment loaded after dark and departed to hit the shore on the Vineyard at first light. Dramatically, the boats came out of the murky light in silence, due to offshore winds. In perfect formation the first wave plowed through the surf and hit the beach exactly at H-hour. Wave after wave of troops swarmed ashore as paratroopers dropped behind the beach to support the landings. The LCVs, LCMs and LCTs (landing craft, vehicle, mechanized, tank) unloaded tons of actual material.[156]

The report concluded, "In its first test, the concept of amphibious invasion was a success."

———

Although the invasion was supposedly cloaked in secrecy, Vineyarders knew what was going on. Galluzzo continued: "Even though the exercise was classified, many people from the Vineyard were out to see it."[157]

A film clip of the invasion was included in a video made by Cimino. He described a "very secret mission. The boats crossed the Sound under tremendous secrecy and the cover of darkness and arrived by dawn or first light. They hit the beach, the boats opened and the troops came ashore. Everything went according to plan." An amused voice-over observes that "most of the population of Martha's Vineyard rose up from the sand dunes and cheered the approaching troops, so the event was not quite as secret as one hoped."[158]

———

Across Vineyard Sound, the *Falmouth Enterprise*, edited by George Hough, Henry Beetle Hough's elder brother, reported, "Once the invasion got underway, there was no halting of the terrific arrival of the infantry men, who, after debarking from their craft, charged forward to contact the enemy in the face of withering machinegun fire and ceaseless bombing from enemy aircraft."[159] (The *Enterprise*'s story was approved by the War Department, written in conjunction with Camp Edwards.)

Soldiers stormed three beachheads to capture Martha's Vineyard. Aircraft dropped practice bombs. Parachutists seized Katama Airport. Medical units swarmed in. Supplies were landed. Chemical warfare troops dropped smoke bombs. Troops established communications and disrupted the enemy.

————

This time, Henry Beetle Hough of the *Vineyard Gazette* gained permission to cover the invasion. The *Gazette* captured the beachhead landing: "Down clanked the jaw-like doors and on to the mushy white sands leaped the infantrymen."[160] The newspaper report continued:

> *Dawn was breaking. The assault boats were now visible in a long, endless line as they ploughed through the choppy waters of the Sound. More troops landed. Soon larger barges could be seen through the early morning haze. They roared up to the beach, unloaded their cargo and disappeared into the morning grey. Still more troops came.*
>
> *…Thousands of Camp Edwards amphibious and amphibian troops stormed across Vineyard Sound in assault boats, invaded the Island of Martha's Vineyard, smashed enemy obstructions, disrupted enemy communications, and forced the foe back into the sea in the most extensive land and sea maneuvers ever staged in this part of the country.*[161]

The story of the military incursion was extensive. "Wave after wave of amphibious infantrymen stormed the Island at three different points, parachute troops seized the vital enemy held airport at Edgartown and aided the invaders in establishing a grip on the Island," reported the *Gazette*.

"After two days, the operation was called to a halt and pronounced a success. General McNair, the man who oversaw the invasion, returned to Washington with the firm conviction that the Army had found the one link that was needed to carry the attack to the enemy—the fast, accurate, and hard-hitting Amphibious Engineers."[162] In their mobile landing craft, the engineers proved key to the success of a landing operation.

General Lesley J. McNair was quoted as saying that "the Martha's Vineyard war games were the most impressive he had ever witnessed."

————

Aqua Cheetah. "I remember the duck boats they had. It was the first one we ever saw," recalled Bob Tilton. "They used to come in, about a foot high out of the water. They used to bring big shots over to the island, perhaps from Camp Edwards. They'd drive right down the sound and across to West Chop." *Courtesy of the National Archives and John Galluzzo.*

Bob Tilton of Vineyard Haven recalls the arrival of General McNair in an Aqua Cheetah, an original "duck" or amphibian boat/car. "I knew it was some kind of a big shot in the jeep. He kept coming once a week or so. We found out it was General McNair, who was the commander and officer of the invasion, either North Africa or someplace." In the invasion of Martha's Vineyard, General McNair stayed at the Ephriam Allen house, courtesy of George Hough.

During the Normandy invasion in 1944, General McNair was killed by friendly fire when a bomb landed in his foxhole.

Toward the end of the mock invasion, the *Gazette* reported, "At long last the chatter of the machine guns was silenced. Raiding parties had completed their mission. And quite effectively. The infantrymen were charging inland now. Engineers were demolishing all enemy barriers and repairing and establishing roads for equipment which soon was to roll off the approaching barges."[163] The next stage of the invasion was underway as the invaders moved inland.

Descriptions of the invasion proved eerily similar to accounts of the landing at Normandy twenty months later.

This second invasion involved more boats, more troops and more activity across the island. "Altogether the amphibious infantrymen, ferried by the engineer amphibians, had made landings and secured high ground south of Norton Beach and east of Lambert's Cove, Sachem's Spring and Chappaquonsett Pond, south of Paul's Point, north of Keephickon (Cape Higgon) and North Tisbury."[164] Martha's Vineyard played an integral role in the training missions that preceded the Normandy invasion.

"The lessons learned from the execution of this second maneuver" improved with "more accurate planning, better timing and coordination, more discipline on the part of troops."[165]

The final evaluation concluded that "everyone connected with the Amphibious Training Center freely admitted that there was room for improvement, and better things were expected when the Center moved to Carrabelle."[166]

Other invasions of Martha's Vineyard followed, but none so dramatic as the first two.

Bill Hannah recalled landings on South Beach, "similar to those done at Normandy months later. They had Higgins boats. They called them the matchbox fleet."[167]

The invasions made an impression on the townspeople. Connie Frank recalled

> *waking up one morning and my father had this wonderful garden on the corner of State Road and Look Street. There were men crawling through the vegetable garden doing maneuvers. It was really eerie. I would say there were fifteen to twenty soldiers crawling on their stomachs. It was weird. It was hard to tell if they were in uniform or not as it was dawn. It was foggy. The garden is still there. It's a good thing my dad didn't see them or he'd be really upset with them rummaging around. I was afraid to tell him. This was in 1943. I just went back to bed. I don't think there were rifles with them.*

Charlotte Meyer recalled:

> *We were sitting on the beach. I remember it like it happened yesterday. And all of a sudden these boats came along and these doors in the front would open up and these soldiers stepped out.* [LSTs were used to transport soldiers.] *We knew the war was on and there were submarines in the waters.*
>
> *I was on the beach with my brother and mother and aunt. My aunt yelled out, "Look at that! Look at that!" as we were sitting on the beach. We saw this boat landing. And I remember seeing men getting off, someone shouting how they were going to go and the men falling into formation. It definitely happened.*
>
> *At first I thought it was a mirage. It was a shock.*

Donald Billings said, "We saw the amphibious boats come into the harbor at the Oak Bluffs dock. Bow drops down. They practiced maneuvers at South Beach."

"I remember watching some practice runs in Vineyard Haven Harbor," recalled Rosalie Powell. "I know they came ashore on the north shore, up near Cape Higgon. Then they got into some of the Chilmark swamps, so they were in tough territory as they tried to get through all the green briars." She continued, "Everybody went to see these LSTs with the ramp which went down. The soldiers and jeeps came ashore. They gathered and then marched somewhere. It was a big production. We were all very impressed and excited about this war thing."

Bob Tilton recalled, "One woman called my father and said, 'Donald, I don't know what is going on up here but some big machine just went through my backyard.' As it turned out, it was a tank. They were all over the place."

Years afterward in *Once More the Thunderer*, a biography of his life as editor of the *Gazette*, Henry Beetle Hough reminisced on the invasion:

> *Then we saw a different sort of home front. An Army captain called up from Camp Edwards and said there would soon be troop maneuvers on and around the Vineyard, and the public should be prepared to take such occurrences as a matter of course. We concluded later that he expected us to print a small item. We surprised him—we made the news our lead story. But no harm was done.*[168]

He added, "Soon a fleet of invasion craft wore through Vineyard Sound and amphibian troops landed at three white beaches in the early morning and took our Island while small groups of civilians looked on from the hills."

Cimino reflected, "Less than a year after the first formation, the 1st Engineer Amphibian Brigade was hitting the beach, first in North Africa, then into southern Italy. Six months later they were coming ashore in Normandy."[169]

———

A later invasion was reported in the *Gazette*: "Hostile Forces are to attack the Vineyard this coming Sunday, May 16, 1943. State Guardsmen are to be in combat position, wearing steel helmets and fatigues, their uniform is Khaki, with regulation shoes and leggings, Khaki cap, coveralls or dungarees."[170] National Guardsmen from Massachusetts, Connecticut and Rhode Island were to participate.

Another newspaper report described a staged attack:

> *Vineyard Haven village echoes with the sound of gunfire as the Tisbury company of State Guards, led by Capt. Hollis Smith, defended the place against an attack led by the Army unit from the Peaked Hill post. Smoke bombs, flares, rockets and sirens were all employed. Plus flour bag grenades, gave the action a touch of realism not easily obtained in the usual small maneuver.*[171]

The exercise was held at night in a drizzly rain, but the atmosphere did little to dampen the enthusiasm of the state guards, who "crawled thru shrubbery and lurked behind hedges"[172] to secure their sites and guard their property. It was a fitting conclusion to the invasions of the Vineyard.

———

"During World War II, while training was underway for the invasion of France, practice landings were made on the northwest shore of the Island near Lambert's Cove," wrote Henry Scott, who served as lieutenant commander at the airfield. "Units of the US Army swarmed ashore from LCIs (landing craft, infantry) in a mock invasion. Army men came through Seven Gates, helmeted and firing weapons at the imaginary enemy." He continued, "By nightfall, pup tents and campfires were everywhere and from behind trees and stone walls wolf calls and whistles were heard whenever the men caught sight of the Flannery girls."[173] The Flannery property had been selected for the invaders' campsite.

"The 'invaders' remained for a few nights and then returned to the landing craft. Some of the officers were happy to spend the night inside the house to avoid the chill air. This being a somewhat secret or 'classified' operation the troops were not permitted to go into the towns." Scott added, "There were also several practice invasions conducted at Wasque on Chappaquiddick."[174]

Another practice drill was held when "fifteen saboteurs were landed on the Island, each charged with a mission of destruction."[175] State guards did not know about this until after the troops had landed.

> *The guardsmen moved out and went into action, with extremely good results as viewed from a military point of view. The guard headquarters at Vineyard Haven were bombed. The court house and telephone exchange at Edgartown were destroyed. But the banks, telephone office at Vineyard Haven, Civilian Defense Headquarters and post offices were all protected, and the saboteurs were all captured, many of them before they had accomplished anything.*[176]

This was a drill for the men of the state guard, who were informed "merely as to how the invaders would be dressed." The article concluded, "Altogether, the observers expressed themselves as being well pleased by the Island demonstration."[177]

Later in the war, the *Gazette* noted that the peak of training at Camp Edwards on Cape Cod had been in the late summer of 1942. "The mock invasion of Martha's Vineyard in October, 1942 was 'the climax of the amphibious season in Cape waters and the large scale dress rehearsal of real invasions to come.'"[178]

CHAPTER 21

NAVY ACQUISITIONS: 1943

The *Vineyard Gazette* welcomed the new year of 1943 with a challenge: "Draw in your belts—1943 is here! This is to be the year of shorter rations and harder work—but the strange part of it is that everyone seems to look forward to it eagerly."[179]

In 1943, the navy assumed ownership of property on Martha's Vineyard and put it directly into military use. Headlines declared: "Navy takes part of Squibnocket Pond for Duration."[180] The navy sought to use the largest freshwater pond on the Vineyard as "a practice bombing target area for the training of fleet combat pilots and bombardiers." Small cast-iron bombs with a charge of black powder would be dropped to emit a puff of smoke "so that the bombardier may see and evaluate his hits. These bombs do not explode with any considerable force and are not dangerous to personnel unless they land very close." Another type of bomb, filled with water, burst on impact. Such bombs were dangerous only if they hit someone. Vineyarders were requested to refrain from frequenting Squibnocket Pond.[181]

By year's end, headlines read, "Navy Takes Noman's." The article recounted that "Noman's Land, long the scene of adventure and romance in fiction and in fact, will play a part in the present war."[182] Three miles long, Noman's Land stands off the southwestern peninsula of Martha's Vineyard. An aircraft target was built by Seabees, who also constructed eleven Quonset huts.[183]

The navy quartered thirty-six enlisted men in the Quonset huts, assigned to tend two targets, nicknamed Meat-Ball and Excelsior, one for five-inch rockets from planes and the other for .50-caliber machine gun strafing. Bombing was carefully monitored. "The rockets used in practice were not explosive and simply tore up the ground."[184]

"On a hill on the island [Noman's] there was a radio shack, two huts for spotting and recording hits on the targets, plus several Quonset huts for housing, mess and recreation," wrote Henry Scott.[185] The navy opened the bombing range in 1944. (Noman's continued to be used for target bombing practice until 1996.)

Another site the navy used was at Tisbury Great Pond, according to the U.S. Army Corps of Engineers. Between 1943 and 1947, Tisbury Great Pond was used for practice dive bombing and strafing. The site supported the navy's fighter training program at Quonset Point and the airfield on Martha's Vineyard. During the initial operational period of the range, strafing and masthead targets were constructed to allow student pilots to develop their gunnery and bombing skills.[186]

Practice ordnance included .30- and .50-caliber ammunition, miniature practice bombs and three-hundred-pound "general purpose bombs." Tisbury Great Pond was not used to store or dispose of munitions.

CHAPTER 22

MARTHA'S VINEYARD NAVAL AUXILIARY AIR FACILITY

A naval air station was built at Quonset Point, Rhode Island; the first plane landed there in December 1940. Quonset Point was headquarters for satellite sites serving Charlestown, Rhode Island; and Hancock, Maine, as well as Martha's Vineyard. These three airfields were built with similar plans, although each had individual tasks.

The navy's primary objectives for planes flying from these bases were to attack enemy submarines and protect convoys headed to Europe.

———

By early 1942, the War Department viewed the four-thousand-acre state forest in the middle of Martha's Vineyard as a potential site for a satellite airfield. The area was relatively flat, without houses nearby. The land had been set aside years earlier as a preserve for the endangered heath hen. However, the last heath hen had died in 1933.

The Dukes County commissioners collaborated with the planning, development and construction of the auxiliary air facility. Their report concluded: "It can be conservatively said this Air Facility will be a most important public improvement and will mean much to the future development of the town of Edgartown and the other municipalities of the county."[187] The county commissioners' suggestion proved correct.

There were no hearings; the navy purchased the property from the State of Massachusetts. The *Gazette* brusquely reported the transaction: "Land

Martha's Vineyard Naval Auxiliary Air Facility. This aerial photo, taken February 21, 1944 from one thousand feet, shows the barracks, hangar, administration building and entrance roadway. The navy marked it confidential, but it was later declassified. *Courtesy of National Archives, College Park, MD.*

acquisition for the air field—683 acres transferred from state to feds for one dollar." Plans for construction were approved, and the proposed facility was to be built with a sense of urgency. The land was surveyed in August 1942. During the war, the airfield was referred to as the Martha's Vineyard Naval Auxiliary Air Facility (MVNAAF). The current name is the Martha's Vineyard Airport.

Island surveyor Hollis Smith once told Jay Schofield that when he was surveying the potential MVNAAF project, he noticed a few minor hummocks and dips in the land. He almost convinced the officials he could straighten the bumps using "contour jacks." Of course, there was no such thing as a contour jack. When he finally let on they needed a bulldozer, everyone had a good laugh.

The contract called for a $1 million facility. Construction provided one hundred jobs for six months for local laborers. It was a challenge to convert

Official navy photographs of planes at the Naval Auxiliary Air Facility, published on the front page of the *Vineyard Gazette*, May 4, 1945. *Courtesy of Hilary Wall and Steve Durkee of the Vineyard Gazette.*

a forested field into a full-fledged military base. Base security came first, including a chain-link fence surrounding the square mile of the government-appropriated airfield.

In September 1942, work began on the airfield at a revised cost of $2 million. The MVNAAF was self-sustaining, with bachelor officers' quarters, barracks for enlisted men, a mess hall, a hospital, shops, a fire department, a water supply, a pumping station and a power plant, as well as a central administration building. It was intended to house two squadrons of fliers. A skeet and pistol range, Link trainer and other programs were planned.

To provide airfield access, roadways from steamship docks had to be revised, as military traffic would be slowed by existing roads. At that time, the current Barnes Road, from the roundabout to the Airport Business Park, did not exist. Sanderson Road was the primary route: into the state forest, to the Manuel Correllus house and then right to the deer-checking station. A now nonexistent road continued to the airport. Hector Asselin recalled, "[We] took the sandy lane that went from Goodale's Pit to the base at the airport. That was the only entrance from the north."[188]

At the outset of World War II, Albion Alley was too old to enlist. He was hired as a guard for the new facility and left his Alley's Store in West Tisbury. Eventually, he became chief of guards at the airfield. A function of the guards was to patrol the fence that surrounded the airfield twice a day. Christian Waller researched the background of the MVNAAF and reported that it used "enough barbed wire to stretch the length of the Vineyard two or three times."[189]

Rugged winter weather early in 1943 delayed work on the airfield. Donald Billings recalled, "A lot of island guys worked at building the airfield. Very rough winter in 1943. My uncle Sam told me they had some tough days because everything was out in the open. Lot of them got pneumonia."

By March, the weather had broken, and construction moved forward with ten-hour workdays. The *Gazette* reported, "The airfield on the central plain of Martha's Vineyard is beginning to shape up as something more than raw earth, mud, and the destination of building materials trucked over the roads from the steamboat landing."[190] The airfield was commissioned on March 26, 1943.

The navy planned to christen the new airport, but "a small, sputtering Army plane" landed first, much to the chagrin of the navy. The following week, the *Gazette* allayed fears when it reported, "It was a Navy plane after all!"[191]

The Avenger torpedo bomber weighed 15,536 pounds fully loaded. It had four machine guns, as well as the capacity to bomb. *Courtesy of the Quonset Air Museum; photo by Thomas Dresser.*

The Avenger flew out of the MVNAAF; it was built by the Grumman Corporation. *Courtesy of the Quonset Air Museum; photo by Thomas Dresser.*

The MVNAAF, like other navy airfields of the era, was designed to accommodate 5,000 military personnel; the island version, however, housed 104 officers and 678 enlisted men.

Ed Krickorian recalled his introduction to the airfield: "I enlisted March 17, 1942. I was seventeen, young as could be."[192]

On his way to the airfield, he was the only passenger on the ferry and the only one on the navy bus, and no one was on the streets of Oak Bluffs. It was January 1943. "When I first came to Martha's Vineyard, I thought they'd put me in no man's land. 'What did I do to deserve this?' It actually was the best thing that ever happened to me."[193]

He got his orders, his barracks, his bunk and his locker and settled in to navy life at the airport. "The barracks were two-story, with double bunks, lockers and a huge bathroom with three or four showers and so many johns. Then after the war they became chicken coops."[194]

Krickorian recalled, "Each unit had mechanics and everybody, radiomen and everything. They stuck together all the time, so they knew each other. I knew everybody on the base. It's like any other base;

The airfield hangar under construction. Local workers completed construction of the airfield, already bustling with navy fliers. *Courtesy of Herb Foster.*

Above: Steel hangars stood behind the planes. Nearby, runways of 3,765, 3,500 and 3,200 feet formed a massive triangle at the airfield. Runways were marked the length of an aircraft carrier for practice landings. *Courtesy of Herb Foster.*

Below: "Our squadron VS 33 was decommissioned at midnight on May 31, 1944," wrote Joseph McLaughlin, "because the Navy felt the submarine danger was over. But that was not the case, because a year later, in May 1945, the *U-853* was sunk by the Navy off the coast of Rhode Island." *Courtesy of Joseph McLaughlin.*

there's pranksters, jokesters, and everybody got along pretty good." He continued: "I was a fireman first class. I shoveled coal to keep the steam up. That's how they heated the airbase, with steam pipes under the ground and old-fashioned radiators, and you also needed steam for cooking and stuff like that."[195]

Another recruit, Hector Asselin, experienced the new airfield as well: "The thing was so new, the bunk beds weren't even set up. They were in these cardboard boxes. Here we were, now toward the end of the day— tired, ragged, our bus burned up, and we had to open up these cardboard cartons in those bare rooms and make our beds."[196]

Initially, pilots at the airfield were trained to attack German submarines torpedoing convoys loaded with supplies for the Allies. According to radioman Joe McLaughlin, the training objective changed during the course of the war. He recalled, "I believe we were the only squadron to patrol for

VS-33

Above: A display case at the Martha's Vineyard airport features mementos from flying exercises during the war. *Photo by Joyce Dresser.*

Left: VS-33 was Joseph McLaughlin's squadron of flyers; their mission was to attack German submarines. *Courtesy of Joseph McLaughlin.*

subs out of the naval base at Martha's Vineyard. After we left, the navy used the place as a training field for pilots who were headed for carrier duty."

Prior to being airborne, pilots experienced the effects of flying in an artificial unit. "These Link trainers look like embryonic planes, hooked up with apparatus from a futuristic movie."[197] Radiomen referenced codebooks, and gunners cooped in tiny turrets practiced target shooting; bombardiers dropped bombs.

The MVNAAF served as a training facility for fighter pilots to learn to take off and land on a runway marked off to be the length of an aircraft carrier. Pilots and crew of navy fighters and bombers underwent a six-week course in the final phase of training before being assigned to aircraft carriers in the Pacific theater.

One exercise required pilots to learn "touch and go" skills. This drill simulated a pilot briefly landing on a carrier and then taking off immediately in case the landing went awry; they learned to abort in seconds. Another exercise was the "bounce" drill, which began with a pilot's very low approach to simulate flying over the ocean to land on the carrier. Bounce drills required long runways. Pilots flew close to the ground so they could land on the lane marked as a designated landing area, as if it were an aircraft carrier.

"There are carrier decks painted on the runways at the NAAF and for a while he'll use these instead of the real thing. The normal approach by a carrier plane is parallel to the carrier but in the opposite direction, down wind, until a point is reached about abreast of the mid-ship section of the vessel."[198]

Joseph Stiles recalled the airfield: "On the base we had fighter planes, we had torpedo bombers, and dive bombers up there." Planes included the Avenger; the Corsair; the Grumman F4 Wildcat, "a short-wing, fighter plane, a good little plane"; and "tough planes, too. An F6-F Grumman Hellcat was the fastest plane the Navy had in those days."[199]

Primary goals of the airfield were to train torpedo fighter pilots in night attacks and to practice aircraft carrier landing. Search and rescue planes were dispatched following crashes. MVNAAF was a busy place. Eleven squadrons flew out of the base in 1943, the first year it opened; fifty squadrons called it home in 1944 and nine in the last year of the war. At its peak, sixty-eight planes were housed at the base.

Another skill taught at the MVNAAF was recognition training, the identification of enemy ships and planes, which became a primary educational goal of the MVNAAF. Pilots learned to identify Japanese and German planes based on models of the real ones supplied by the Van Ryper shop in Vineyard Haven. Training included a rheostat to simulate bright morning sun or evening light. Pilots learned to identify silhouettes of enemy aircraft and ships.

Hector Asselin was in charge of training the MVNAAF recognition class. Additionally, he served as the movie projectionist on base. He set up a theater

Grumman F6F Hellcats flying in tandem. Prior to President Clinton's first presidential vacation, in 1993, the coast guard discovered a submerged Hellcat off Cape Poge in an aerial survey of Vineyard waters. *Image on display at Martha's Vineyard Airport; photo by Joyce Dresser.*

in Barracks Three I think it was. The upper floor was empty and we had a bigger screen, and some seats that were not folding seats. They were comfortable seats. We set them up there and oh, boy!

It was a happy sort of a condition there. And word came that Quonset was sending over 35mm projectors, the real theater projectors, and going to send over films that came right out of Hollywood! Well, Clark Gable was in the first picture and it was current, it was just a late release.[200]

Sailors brought their girlfriends back to the base to watch the movies. It became very popular.

An accident occurred at the MVNAAF, and two men died in a gas tank. "One man gave his life in a vain attempt to save another, and three other men risked their lives in an effort to rescue two men attached to the MVNAAF from a huge gas tank Monday afternoon, after they had been overcome by gas fumes."[201]

A plaque placed by Ed Krickorian by the entrance to the Martha's Vineyard Airport recognizes two men who died in the tragic 1944 gas tank accident. *Photo by Joyce Dresser.*

Ed Krickorian, a fireman at the airfield, recalled that fateful day of January 17, 1944. Richard Holden, age twenty-one, was a water tender. Along with "a fellow named Goodwin," he had descended a ladder into the gas tank to measure how much fuel remained. Goodwin felt faint and climbed out, inadvertently kicking the ladder. Holden never made it out. Another man, William Ping, jumped into the tank to try to rescue Holden. Krickorian let himself down into the tank to try to find Holden.

Standing on the floor of the tank with gasoline up to his chest and a rope round his waist, Krickorian felt a body at the bottom of the tank, reached down and hauled it up. Krickorian survived, but both Richard Holden and William Ping died.

Krickorian recovered and was deployed on a destroyer to the Pacific. "Everybody that knew anything about this incident got shipped out,"[202] he recalled.

CHAPTER 23

PLANE CRASHES: 1944

I remember all kinds of plane crashes," recalled Hector Asselin. "Oh, there was a lot of life lost. We had night patrol squadrons go out and some of the planes never got back. In fact, just recently [interviewed in 2002], they found one of the planes off-shore and they keep finding them, you know, as the dredgers go out."[203]

Training accidents were common. "Forty Vineyard [MVNAAF] trainees died in the twenty months between the first crash (the week of September 19, 1943) and the last (the week of May 11, 1945), two or three or even six at a time, many killed in crashes within sight of the island, and most at the age of twenty or twenty-one.'"[204]

Pilots could not use their radios while approaching the blacked-out Vineyard, which proved a problem for night flying. A plane would run out of fuel with the pilot unaware of where he was and would crash.

"As part of all that nighttime stuff, many of the navy planes would drop flares, maybe to look for other navy planes that crashed," recalled Jane Slater. "Many nights were lit up with the flares, three or four at a time, in the air. Next day, I'd get to go look for the parachute; we'd just love those parachutes. We'd spend hours picking the parachutes out of the *Rosa rugosa* because we wanted them perfect."

Everett Poole said, "The coast guard was very busy with all the planes that were crashing. They would drop parachute flares to find the pilot. My cousin and I went out to collect the parachutes. We'd sell the chutes to lobstermen for their pots and sold the nylon to a dressmaking shop in Vineyard Haven. We made some good money."

Asselin recalled: "I had a close call. I was on duty in a new jeep patrolling the air base. My crew did pretty much the same thing. We wound up on patrol at the airbase." Asselin was driving outside the chain-link fence of the airbase from Edgartown toward West Tisbury. "I heard sirens as I'm driving along, and I said, 'Something's wrong,' but I couldn't see anything. This plane came in, its wheels were down, and hit the top of the fence, right over my head, and landed upside down. I stopped. And I was on the wrong side of the fence." The plane flipped, but the pilot managed to open the canopy and get out. "He was dazed, and everyone was coming at him. He was able to get out." That day, three planes went out and only one came back.

"And squadrons from Quonset would come in and fly over to the Vineyard for relaxation," Asselin recalled. A family came to congratulate their son. "It was the morning. Their son had signed out a plane, a TBF (torpedo bomber fighter). I was standing there. And he went round once, and right in front of them, he went right down. He just dropped. I was right there."

A lot was happening all across Martha's Vineyard. In the two years the MVNAAF functioned during the war, planes crashed on takeoff or landing or, more likely, in night flights and practice bombing runs. "Then there were those heartbreaking days in early 1945 when plane after plane flew in night training from the new field and crashed inexplicably in the sea. Between February and April, fifteen airmen were lost, and almost as many planes."[205] A light switch failed, making night flying a challenge.

Jane Slater recalled one crash:

> *My grandmother liked to stay up late at night. One night, a plane flew over the house and she watched it crash into Dogfish Bar. It had lights on, and the lights illuminated the Lobsterville Beach, so she knew exactly where it went down. And she called the coast guard to tell them where she saw the plane crash. The next day, we had very big army brass come to the house and they asked what she saw. It was a very serious thing to them, and they didn't want us to talk about it. I always wondered about it. Many years later, long after the war, the army did come and get it [the plane].*

A Corsair carrier plane from the MVNAAF was found off Dogfish Bar in July 1958 in thirty-two feet of water. Human bones were in the cockpit. No other information was revealed. This likely was the plane Jane Slater's grandmother saw go down.[206]

One airman, Joseph McLaughlin, shared the drama of a first-person account flying over the waters of Martha's Vineyard when the engine died:

Before the navy made the base at Martha's Vineyard, we flew out of Quonset Point. On this patrol, we were out about one hundred miles when the plane engine started to miss and the whole plane was shaking. My pilot, Lieutenant West, called me on the intercom and said we were headed back and we might have to ditch the plane on the way in.

So he dropped the depth charges and brought the plane down to just a few hundred feet above the water and headed for Martha's Vineyard. I threw the codebook over the side of the plane. The codebook had metal covers so that as soon as it hit the water it went down. We had lost sight of our wing plane due to low clouds and tried to call them but did not make contact. So he told me to use the telegraph key and tell the base we were headed back. Just about then the radio cut out, so we were on our own. We flew for what seemed an eternity and finally sighted Martha's Vineyard. Then we ran into a small storm of rain and snow and could just about see, but Lieutenant West managed to set the plane down.

I'm not sure if it was a runway or a road, but just after we landed, the engine stopped. He told me to stay with the plane, and he started out on foot to find a house with a telephone. He had walked about a mile, then saw an old man with a rifle walking towards him. For a few moments, he thought he might be shot. The old man asked him if he needed help. Lieutenant West told him our problem, so the old man walked him to the nearest house with a phone, and he called the base to get help. While he was in the house, the lady there made up some sandwiches and some hot coffee for us both. Eventually, the plane was fixed and we returned to base.

————

Following is a list of plane crashes with location and survival information:

AUGUST 31, 1943: Three died when two navy planes from Quonset collided over Nashawena. Three men parachuted and were rescued. "The accident was observed by eyewitnesses on Cuttyhunk."[207]

OCTOBER 22, 1943: Three planes from the MVNAAF disappeared on a night flight and six men were missing. "If the men are not found the Island airfield will have sustained its first major disaster. Up to now there have been accidents to planes, as in all training centers, but no loss of life."[208] All six flyers died in the crash.

December 24, 1943: A plane crashed off the south shore of the Vineyard, but it was "not from the Island field."[209]

January 28, 1944: A pilot was saved when his plane crashed in the scrub oak trees of West Tisbury, nearly a mile from the airfield. The plane was demolished, but the pilot walked away.

March 18, 1944: A single NAAF plane went down off Edgartown, but there was neither injury nor damage to the plane.

April 14, 1944: Three men in a torpedo bomber survived a crash in the state forest.

April 21, 1944: Two planes crashed over Nantucket. Three flyers were lost, a parachutist drowned and one man in his rubber boat was rescued.

June 2, 1944: On a routine training flight from New Bedford, a navy Avenger torpedo bomber "suddenly plunged into the water off West Chop, carrying its crew of three to their deaths."[210]

July 28, 1944: A pilot landed safely in the scrub brush of West Tisbury. His plane was wrecked, but he walked away. (This may be the crash Hector Asselin witnessed.)

August 18, 1944: A flyer crashed near Edgartown on a training mission. The plane went under water, and the pilot was stuck beneath the cowl (windshield frame) but used a hand-crank to open it. "He wore a Mae West which kept him afloat, but the rubber emergency boat failed to inflate automatically, and he blew it up himself, by mouth, while floating in the seas."[211] He was rescued by a coast guard boat from Vineyard Haven.

September 1, 1944: A pilot from MVNAAF flew to Menemsha to rescue an injured man, and "he set down the little ship with the greatest of ease, but not without exciting the admiration of everyone who saw or knows the landing field he used, the beach, in the scanty space between the water and the rip-rapping."[212]

October 6, 1944: Five men died when two torpedo bombers collided south of Nantucket. Coast guard and navy personnel assisted in the search, but there was no trace of the men.

November 24, 1944: One pilot died in a collision over Nashawena.

December 29, 1944: Three flyers were rescued off the south shore. Young boys witnessed the crash. The flyers launched their rubber raft. Larry Mercier recalled, "I told you about the story of my brother and Tom and Harry Flynn. They saw that plane go down and had enough sense to go back to the house and make calls and save everybody."

January 12, 1945: A pilot was injured when his torpedo bomber went down in Christiantown.

JANUARY 26, 1945: Three flyers died off Gay Head, a mile out to sea. They were in a torpedo bomber on a training mission at night. No survivors were found.

FEBRUARY 7, 1945: A pilot crash-landed between two houses and a stone wall in Orlin F. Davis's field in Chilmark (see report in the next section).

FEBRUARY 16, 1945: Pilot Ted Hall of Edgartown died in a plane crash in the woods near the airfield. From the control tower, it was observed that he was having difficulties; he tried to jump, but his chute "didn't blossom."

FEBRUARY 23, 1945: A plane disappeared, and the pilot was missing.

MARCH 1, 1945: A navy torpedo bomber crashed off Edgartown, and three men died.

MARCH 2, 1945: A crash killed three flyers in night training.

MARCH 9, 1945: A plane crashed into Lambert's Cove, but the pilot was rescued.

MARCH 16, 1945: Flares ignited fires on the West Tisbury–Chilmark town line.

MARCH 16, 1945: A navy plane landed off Noman's; the pilot suffered minor injuries.

APRIL 13, 1945: A pilot was rescued off Cape Pogue.

MAY 11, 1945: A pilot died when his plane exploded after a bounce drill at the MVNAAF. (This may have been the second crash Hector Asselin saw.)

Everett Poole, a teenager in Chilmark during the war, was part of the action.

On February 16, 1945 Bert Cahoon, Daniel Manter and Albion Alley received letters of thanks and commendation for the immediate and timely aid they rendered to a pilot of a plane forced down on the Orlin Davis property on Middle Road in Chilmark last week.[213]

More than sixty years later, Everett Poole notified John Alley, son of Albion, that he still had a piece of the propeller from this plane in his chandlery shop in Menemsha.

Poole recalls more wartime activity. "During and after the war, smoke bombs and rockets were dropped by planes on practice targets on Noman's Land, in the Great Ponds and Squibnocket."

He has another story:

One day when there was a plane crash, and they had to take all the personnel from the coast guard station in Gay Head. But the fishermen were supposed to check with the coast guard as to when and where they were going out. Nobody was around in Menemsha, so the coast guard grabbed me and told me to check the boats in and out because they all had to go out to look for the downed pilot. I was twelve years old.

The lifeboat came back with the pilot. Soon afterward, several commissioned officers arrived. One of them was a captain, a four-striper. He came up to me and asked, "Where's the watch man?"

"One of those planes [from the airfield] crashed in Orlin Davis's field in Chilmark," recalled Everett Poole. "It was wrecked." He added, "I have a piece of the propeller." *Photo by Thomas Dresser.*

"He's out in one of the boats," I said. I was checking in a fishing boat at the time.

"What are you doing there?" he queried.

I said, "They didn't have anybody else to check in the boats."

Then he said, "We can't have a kid checking in the boats."

I told him there was nothing to it and showed him my clipboard, where I just checked them off.

"You're doing a good job," he replied.

The MVNAAF salvaged crashed planes and brought them to Oak Bluffs Harbor, where they were sent off by barge. Donald Billings said, "All the stuff came by barge. No ferryboats, only steamers. A guard patrolled the area with the damaged planes. Someone knew the guard, and sometimes he let us kids play in the planes."

Nancy Billings has a ring made from a dime flattened by a machinist at the airfield. "You know, they made a lot of prefab [parts] there for the damaged planes," recalls her husband, Donald.

Then there were the accidents in our harbors and at sea:

JULY 3, 1942: Two patrol torpedo (PT) boats entered Edgartown Harbor. They were known as mosquito boats, "a sufficiently apt title because of the startling way in which they seem to fly up and down in the waves, and the terrific speed of which they are capable."[214] Each vessel was seventy feet long and carried three torpedoes.

"Life aboard a mosquito boat could be recommended only for the young and sound," wrote the *Gazette*. "In addition, the vibration and the sound of the exploding engines is both nerve wracking and deafening. But the P.T. boats deliver the goods and their crews can take it."[215]

JULY 24, 1942: Three weeks later, the *Gazette* was less enthralled. The crew of *C.S. Monitor* dropped a TNT depth charge into Edgartown Harbor. It failed to explode, as it was set in less than thirty feet of water, too shallow to ignite. A week later, a second charge was dropped; both bombs detonated in a great plume of water.

JULY 2, 1943: A tragedy occurred off the south shore. Four EAC (engineer amphibian command) men died in swift currents off Skiffs Island.[216] They had been practicing invasion technique training near Chappaquiddick, and their craft overturned.[217]

JULY 7, 1944: Seven navy men died when a destroyer escort and a minesweeper collided off Cuttyhunk.

CHAPTER 24

EDGAR

The Allies had to invade the continent if they were to defeat the Axis powers. The decision was made to invade North Africa first. That campaign began late in 1942 and concluded in the spring of 1943.

While soldiers were invading North Africa, the War Department devised plans to invade Europe by crossing the English Channel. Military vehicles needed oil and gas. "Without gasoline, a mechanized army could not operate but would be stranded on the coast of Normandy," the *Gazette* explained.[218] A pipeline had to be installed under the English Channel from England to France. To go beneath the English Channel, pipe would run thirty miles and be as much as 150 feet deep.

Two independent enterprises tackled the challenge. A British group was nicknamed Pluto. "British auspices developed a flexible pipe similar to the casing of a submarine electric cable, which could be wound on a drum and floated to sea."[219]

An American plan, devised by Colonel John Leavell, used solid pipe and established a base in Katama. The coastal waters off South Beach resembled those of the English Channel in both depth and current. This secret experiment was code-named Edgar.

The army appropriated the land of a local farmer. The *Vineyard Gazette* challenged the army's method of taking property. "Here's a bit of war news from an unidentified Island off the North Atlantic coast,"[220] the *Gazette* wrote, concealing the identity of the locale but not the farmer, Edward Vincent, age seventy-three:

The Army recently leased and took over some land on this Island, and when soldiers and equipment moved in, a farmer whose land was adjoining, asked how about his cows [sic]. The Army people said that was all right, he could keep his cows where they were and put them out and take them in when he wished. This was in the afternoon. But the next afternoon, going for the cows, which were on land the Army hadn't wanted and hadn't asked for, this farmer was told by a guard that he couldn't go through without a pass. He couldn't get a pass without seeing the lieutenant, and the lieutenant wasn't anywhere around. No one could say when he would be back, either, and it was getting dark and the cows had to be milked.

The guard said that if the farmer tried to go past for his cows, he would be shot, and after a little more time, with the evening coming on, the farmer said all right, the sentry could go ahead and shoot, but he was going for his cows. He went, too, and the sentry did not shoot.[221]

The newspaper added drama to its account, but the point was made.

Once it had the land, the U.S. Army Transportation Corps of the U.S. Army Service Forces began the project in August 1943. "Col. John H. Leavell, an oil operator of long and successful experience, began toying with the idea."[222]

Buildings were constructed. Equipment arrived. A crew from Wright Field, Ohio, flew to Edgartown on September 5, 1943; only key people knew the purpose of the trip.

The signal corps worked at the base with the U.S. Army Corps of Engineers and the navy. After the war, when the project was revealed, the *Gazette* noted, "The Army took drastic steps to insure [*sic*] the secrecy of the operations, and civilians and unauthorized personnel were excluded even from the approaches to the experimental base."[223] Locals knew something was happening but not what. No one could explain the quantity of pipe delivered to the Edgartown pier. Complete secrecy was imposed for the duration of the experiment.

The U.S. Army Corps of Engineers worked with the Atlantic Pipe Line Company. Ten miles of 4.5 OD (outside diameter), extra heavy, straight, steel pipe were delivered. Cranes, trucks and pipe layers were employed; two tugs towed the pipe off South Beach, communicating by radio with shore personnel.

Each section of the five miles of pipe was brought to the beach, and the first section was "towed in to the ocean and stopped so the end could be welded to the second one-mile length. This process continued until the five-mile length was towed into position. When the last mile was added, three tow boats were required to move the five-mile lengths."[224]

The strength of the welded joints was tested as a three-thousand-foot piece of pipe was successfully dragged over a fifty-mile course of ocean water without undo abrasion.

The *Gazette* reported two years later that the project was undertaken "with the aid of tugs, and welded together into an experimental pipeline under conditions similar to those which would be encountered in laying a gasoline supply line under the English channel."[225]

———

Pluto, with flexible, hose-like pipe, was deemed the better model and was approved by the War Department. The line became operational on August 12, 1944, shortly after D-Day. Colonel Leavell believed his system superior because it was made of steel, which permitted higher pressure for a faster force of gasoline.

In his typically breezy phraseology, Henry Beetle Hough summarized the story of Edgar:

> *Few knew the truth until after the end of the war—all that pipe trucked past the security lines to the Great Plain had been dragged across the ocean beach and laid through the surf again and again as tests were made of a plan to lay similar pipe under the English Channel for the pumping of gasoline at the time of the invasion. But the British had also developed such a scheme and theirs was the one used—Operation Pluto of the history books.*[226]

In one of those history books, a German one, former Luftwaffe military aviator Adolf Galland wrote, "Two artificial harbors and a pipeline that had been laid across the Channel allowed the landing of heavy material and the continuous supply of fuel."[227]

Decades later, Christian Waller recounted that the top-secret story of Edgar "added more to the wartime atmosphere that hung over the Island rather than directly changing the way in which people went about their business."[228]

Again, the Vineyard played a role in wartime efforts.

CHAPTER 25

THE GUNNERY RANGE

T he navy needed a firing range for pilots. Again, Katama was selected.
When Henry Beetle Hough learned the navy intended to develop
a firing range right in Edgartown, he was irate and wrote his congressman,
Charles Gifford, who had served in the House of Representatives since
1922. Representative Gifford contacted the navy and received a response.
The navy agreed with concerns raised about a firing range right outside
town, but its letter assured Congressman Gifford it would not create much
noise: "Practically all of the shooting will be done with machine guns or at
most with 20 mm. cannon, which is a small caliber weapon. The disturbance
created by this type of activity will be hardly more than that which is suffered
from a rifle range. We very much doubt if the fire can even be heard in the
village of Edgartown."[229] That did not prove to be the case.

The navy proceeded with plans. Surveyors recorded land bounds from
the Katama airport to South Beach, and the *Gazette* revisited the story of
the farmer.
The navy failed to convey its intentions to Edward Vincent, the above-
named Katama farmer whose seventy-five acres were used for grazing cattle
and harvesting hay. "Nobody has ever said a word to Mr. Vincent," wrote
the *Gazette*, "but when he went down to take a look he discovered a bulldozer
knocking down fence for the distance of a quarter of a mile. He spoke about

An aerial photograph of South Beach, from 1938, where wartime activities occurred. Hollis Smith surveyed the gunnery range. *Courtesy of Russell Smith, grandson of Hollis Smith.*

this to the man in charge who said that if he wanted to keep any of the posts he had better hurry up and get them out of the way."[230] The story continued: "The same man said that if Mr. Vincent wanted to watch [the new] fence which is to be put up, he could tell how much of his land the Navy was going to take."

Mr. Vincent said, "I decided to try to forget about it." The *Gazette* added, presciently, "The taking of the Vincent land also affects the access of the public to the South Beach, which is likely to be cut off entirely for the duration of the war."[231] It was.

The navy developed a gunnery range with a moving target pulled by a train along a track for machine gunners to fire from planes. When not in use, the train was housed in a concrete structure, which became a local landmark on the shore after the war.

Construction of the target range got underway in late November 1943. No one was allowed access to the gunnery range. "I remember you couldn't go to South Beach," said Peg Kelley. "It was off limits because they were practicing dive-bombing." The area was protected by a guardhouse, and the road at the forks was blocked. "Behind the fencing was a highly guarded secret with security stations at the perimeter and 24-hour manned coverage by both the military and the local sheriff's department."[232]

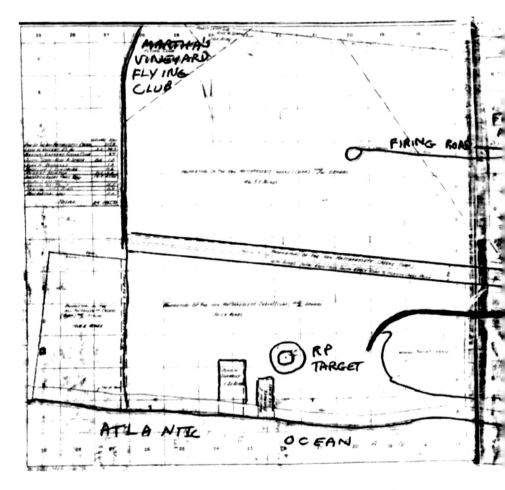

The gunnery range was used for target practice at South Beach. Sand was bulldozed into a long rampart to protect the moving target. Planes strafed the target. *Courtesy of Dave Larsen.*

Veteran Jesse Morgan described the range: "There was a gunnery range where the restaurant is today [in 1988, Edgar's Bar and Grill]. There were rooms and garages. In the garages they had big Mack trucks which carried gun turrets mounted on the back." He continued: "There was a man-made dune. A target ran on a railroad track. The object came out between the dunes. Occasionally a plane towed a target. We shot the heck out of it. Sometimes we shot the plane."[233]

Robert Boren, a coast guardsman who worked on communications at the range, "frequently had to go to South Beach to repair a military telephone

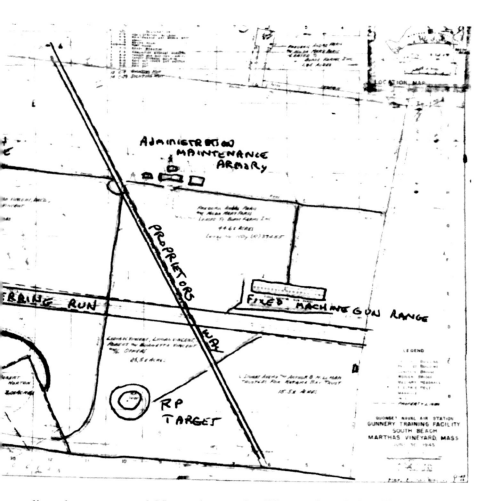

line that connected Nantucket to the Vineyard and the Vineyard to the mainland. The line was damaged regularly by artillery fire." He described the range: "There was a narrow railroad track where they used to run a moving target. A Navy fighter plane would fly in and fire rockets at the sleds they were towing." He added: "They attacked from both ways. They came in over the water and from the land."[234]

He went on: "It was a noisy place. Frequent explosions were heard down at the beach. Low-flying planes regularly strafed targets near the beach." A lot was going on: "The rockets had explosive heads. They had a smoke charge in them to let the pilot know where they hit. It helped the pilot know if he missed the target."

Laurence "Larry" Mercier recalled, "Where they used to shoot, they dug a huge pit. It is still there. That was where they used to do target practice." He went on: "On the beach, they had a concrete embankment; it was huge. It ended up in the ocean. It was concrete-sided and had one concrete partition in it, then the walls, and we would go in there and it was big enough to have a fire—it was unbelievable."

He continued: "When the navy came here, you know where Mattakeesett [Winnetu] is now, those were barracks for the navy. And they did maneuvers on the beach. They were teaching people how to run LCMs and LCUs (landing craft, utility) to the beach."

Chris Kennedy, of the Trustees of Reservations, added: "The loop track constituted the Moving Target Machine Gun Range target track. The 'bunker' was a hardened structure located in the middle of the loop track, used to house the engine which pulled the machine gun target around the track." Everyone associated with the gunnery range remarked on the high level of noise.

Henry Scott recalled plans to expand the target range, but the hurricane of September 1944 interfered: "The railroad was wiped out by the storm. Everyone was surprised by the storm."[235]

John Alley said: "The government built a wooden railroad on the beach. It was at least 150 feet long. Its purpose was to tow targets. They only dropped practice bombs, by the way. After the practice bombing, they'd go out, fix it all up and do it all over again. But that basically got washed out to sea in hurricanes."

CHAPTER 26

SUBMARINES AND SABOTEURS

The word "U-boat" derives from the German word *Unterseeboot*, which means undersea boat, hence "U-Boot" or the English term "U-boat." The infamous U-boats, German submarines, patrolled the waters off Martha's Vineyard during World War II and wrought havoc. They attacked convoys of merchant ships transporting military munitions and tankers bringing fuel oil to Allied forces. Allied ships were sunk by U-boats throughout the war.

Two U-boats were discovered near the Vineyard decades after they were sunk by the Allies. U-boat *550* was sunk seventy miles south of Nantucket on April 16, 1944. The 252-foot submarine had torpedoed the Allied tanker *Pan Pennsylvania*, laden with gasoline and headed for Great Britain. The USS *Joyce*, an escort for the tanker, caught the image of *U-550* on sonar and dropped a depth charge, forcing the sub to surface. The crew of *U-550* had to abandon ship but blew it up prior to escaping. In 2012, the sub was discovered by a privately funded group.

A second German U-boat, *U-853*, lies off Block Island, 130 feet below the surface. "On May 5, 1945, near Point Judith, Rhode Island, the submarine torpedoed and sank the SS *Black Point*, carrying coal from New York to Boston. Twelve men died on the *Black Point*, the last U.S. merchant ship sunk in the Atlantic during the war."[236] The news report added, "Germany's naval authorities had already ordered all U-boats to return home, but the young captain of the *U-853* either ignored or never received the orders."[237] Depth charges sent from the USS *Atherton* and its sister ship,

This German Unterseeboot, *U-1229*, was sunk by torpedo bombers from the USS *Bogue* on August 20, 1944. The U-boat surfaced, and the crew abandoned ship; forty-two Germans were taken prisoners of war off Argentia, Newfoundland. *Courtesy of the Mariners' Museum.*

the USS *Moberly*, sank the *U-853*, and fifty-five German sailors perished. This event took place the day before Nazi Germany surrendered. Because the site of the wreck is a war grave, divers are forbidden to remove or salvage anything from the *U-853*.

"Some nights there was a strange throbbing engine noise clearly heard in our living room," recalled Jane Slater. "Those nights, my grandmother would call the coast guard to report hearing it. They, most often, could hear it too and agreed that most likely, a submarine was surfaced in the lee of Squibnocket and was charging its batteries. This actually happened often."[238] She added to the memory in an interview in 2013: "No one was going to do anything about it. It was the middle of the night. It was impractical to send planes out. They're not going to blow them up in the harbor next to the shore."

This unidentified German U-boat surfaced in the North Atlantic. Submarines were on the minds of Vineyarders during the war. Jane Slater recalled that U-boats lurked off Squibnocket and surfaced at night to charge their batteries. *Courtesy of the Mariners' Museum.*

"There was a terrific undercurrent of mysterious activity," Slater continued. "I don't know how much of it was real and how much wasn't. People would see lights on the cliffs and call the coast guard, and the coast guard would say, 'Yes, we see it.' And yet townspeople were not afraid. They just had to endure it. It was 1944. It was a strange time."

Chilmark resident David Flanders, interviewed in 2000, said, "I've seen German submarines come up and charge their batteries during the War. They'd come up in the lee of the Island here."[239] Flanders thought he discovered a spy hiding out in a beach cottage, communicating with German submarines. Although the FBI was contacted, the fellow got away.

Bud Mayhew added to the story: "David Flanders, my neighbor, heard the German subs surface to recharge their batteries. They would board a dragger to get fish from the fishermen for food." No weapons were shown.

Eric and Marguerite Cottle described rumors of German saboteurs coming ashore and patrols assigned to catch them:

> *Marguerite Cottle: There were the blackouts. You know, it was pretty dismal. Eric was in the fishing industry, and they never called him because they needed the fishermen. Were we allowed on the beaches during the war?*
>
> *Eric Cottle: No, they were patrolled. Patrolled clear around the island as far as I know.*
>
> *MC: The beaches were patrolled by the Coast Guard. And they would take turns coming down through. They were looking for saboteurs all the time. There were always rumors going that they were coming ashore...*
>
> *EC: We had to go to the Coast Guard before we went out, report to them when we come in...*
>
> *MC: It was scary. Of course, I was young, you know, and there were rumors. We never knew what was true and what wasn't because it was just rumors. They claimed that saboteurs were coming ashore.*
>
> *EC: They claimed they did, but I don't know. They sunk one or two submarines off of here, or so they said. Boy, it was some dark. They cut the lighthouse, the power to the lighthouses way down, you could hardly see the lights. You couldn't have any light shining on your windows. It was all blackout curtains. I used to go out and patrol up on the North Road, make sure nobody was on the road who wasn't suppose to be. I'd go up there, sit in the car and see a car coming. I'd stop them. Find out what there were doing out. Had to have special dispensation to get anywhere.*[240]

U-588 torpedoed the unescorted, unarmed *Gulftrade* tanker off the New Jersey shore. This image shows the "aerial starboard bow section of ship sinking after being torpedoed/sunk March 10, 1942." Eighteen men died. U-boats ruled the waves in the first half of 1942. *Courtesy of the Mariners' Museum.*

Jane Slater added, "They always said there was one [saboteur] here. Somebody on this island must know that story. The rubber boat came ashore, way down-island. These guys tried to leave the island on the ferry. And they got caught, that's all I know. I don't know the details."

Joseph Stiles, who was in the navy, recalled:

> *One time my ship came up to the Vineyard. They had a kind of submarine scare around the Vineyard, so three of our ships came up here. We anchored right off the Menemsha and Gay Head area. Our three destroyers boxed the submarine in between Noman's and Gay Head. And then, after three days, we were told to pull out. We didn't know why—they would never tell us anything—but later we found out that the captain of the submarine defected from the German Navy.* [241]

A local physician shared a story he was told happened on the island during the war. Two spies came ashore and were caught and ended up on Paul's Point in West Tisbury. One of them died and is buried there.

Larry Mercier retold an incident that occurred between Gay Head and Block Island. "A German submarine came up alongside [fisherman Louie DeSett,] commandeered all the fuel they had on board, the groceries, whatever they had, and didn't do anything to them. They [the U-boat] just went back down and were never seen again, so they must have been heading back to Germany."

"The Germans had free run of the Atlantic Ocean. They wanted to scope out the airbase, maybe do some sabotage," John Alley said. "They would surface the U-boat, let people out in the rubber raft, come ashore, hide the raft wherever they could as the shore patrol would be around. And they had, I'm sure if they took off their wet suits or whatever they had, they were all dressed in clothing like we would be wearing."

Alley warmed to his account:

A group of them surfaced and ended up at the Menemsha Inn, which was the place to go for dinner in the 1940s. My sister, Phyllis, was a waitress, and she told the story to me. These people seemed suspicious. They came to the Menemsha Inn and were having dinner, and the waitresses were a bit suspicious. It could have been the way they dressed. I'm sure they shed any accent they might have had. What they [the waitresses] were instructed to do was call the shore patrol. The shore patrol came and entered the restaurant. In situations like that, I was told the shore patrol would sort of mingle. They wouldn't be dressed in uniform, of course.

The shore patrol sent for backup and arrested the suspects. Alley believes there were as many as six saboteurs, or spies, but there is no documentation. The saboteurs "didn't have a lot of resources to work with. They didn't have big German cells here. There were a few folks here of German descent, but they were all pro-America." No one knows what happened to the suspects.

Jeanette DiMeglio, who grew up in Germany, shared a recollection. When her elder brother Willie turned eighteen, he joined the German navy. His grandmother didn't want him to go, but he had to.

Several members of the family, including Jeanette, immigrated to the United States. Willie's mother, brothers and aunts relocated to New York City. During the war, three of Willie's brothers—Otto, Oscar and Joe—joined the United States Army. Otto was a chauffeur for General Patton. Willie remained in the German navy.

Jeanette DiMeglio says her brother Willie was in a German submarine, a U-boat, off the shores of Martha's Vineyard. He peered out his periscope, wishing he could escape from the submarine and come ashore onto Martha's Vineyard.

After the war, Willie returned to Heilbronn, West Germany, but kept in touch with Jeanette in the United States.

Rumors flourished that German saboteurs had been set ashore. Saboteurs supposedly debarked from Nazi submarines in small rubber boats on remote Vineyard beaches with the intent of disrupting or destroying American factories or spying on American activities.

"There were so many stories of the possibility of spies," said Jane Slater. "If they [the submarines] came in close enough to charge their batteries, which they had to do, people could communicate with them." She raises the possibility that spies came ashore. "Did they ever launch rubber boats to put people ashore? Everyone's got a story. Up-island, down-island. The topic is ripe for speculation. Supposedly they did put people ashore, and they could assimilate, you see."

The War Department censored the press, so stories of German saboteurs were not publicized. However, three cases of landings on American shores from German U-boats did make the press: one in Florida, another in New York and a third in Maine. There is no documented evidence of a landing by Germans on Martha's Vineyard, although stories persist.

On June 13 and 17, 1942, two groups of German saboteurs landed on American shores. The first, from *U-202*, was at Amagansett, Long Island, and the second, from *U-584*, occurred at Ponte Vedra Beach, Florida. U-boats set four trained Nazi agents ashore at each site; these were sabotage experts who spoke fluent English and were designed to blend in while they pursued nefarious deeds.[242]

Days after the men came ashore, the FBI captured all eight saboteurs. One of their own, Georg Dasch, had turned them in. Six German nationals were tried for espionage and executed. Dasch and another saboteur were American citizens; they were imprisoned and then deported to Germany after the war.

"It appears that most of the incidents were hushed up before they reached the press. Was there a deliberate effort by J. Edgar Hoover and the FBI to prevent the public from knowing the extent of the problem?"[243] The question lingers. "The number of enemy operatives that may have successfully entered the country by submarine or other means is subject to conjecture."[244]

A third documented landing occurred at Hancock Point near Ellsworth, Maine, on November 29, 1944.[245] A pair of Nazi saboteurs rowed ashore off *U-1230* to Mount Desert Island, and shortly thereafter, they were apprehended when they tried to hitchhike to Bangor.[246]

Between 1942 and 1945, nineteen German U-boats were in Vineyard waters. Of those, fifteen U-boats were offshore in 1942. In 1943, one U-boat, *U-161*, was offshore. In 1944, *U-1230* was off the Vineyard. And in 1945, there were two U-boats: *U-879* and *U-853*, which was sunk off Point Judith, Rhode Island.

Records of U-boat activity around Martha's Vineyard were confirmed by a German war records analyst. Thomas Weis wrote in November 2013 from the Library of Contemporary History in Stuttgart, Germany: "Thanks for your requiry. Cape Cod is in position 41°41'N 70°121'W, and that's in naval grid CA 3541. U-Boot activities near Cape Cod are researchable via 8 o'clock position report. As far as I could find out, no spies were landed in the area. There were several attacks in the area CA 3."

Facing is the naval grid that describes U-boat torpedo activity:

ID	ASS P.	DATE	U-BOAT	GRID	CONVOY	TIME	NAT	TYPE	NAME	TONNAGE	POSITION
1515	73	1942-01-14	U-123	CA 3775		0630	pa	-MT	Norness	9577 BRT	40.28n 70.50w
1860	91	1942-04-24	U-576	CA 3975		1230	nw	-D	Tropic Star	5088 BRT	40.50n 68.42w
U-576 heard the torpedo hit, but it was a dud and did not explode. Tropic Star was not damaged.											
1870	92	1942-04-30	U-576	CA 3357		0600	nw	-D	Taborfjell	1339 BRT	41.52n 67.43w
1871	92	1942-04-30	U-576	CA 3358	unknown			-D		5000 BRT	
U-576 fired two torpedoes against four ships overlapping each other and heard one detonation after 6:04 min without optical observation.											
2131	104	1942-06-16	U-87	CA 3268	XB.25	0325	br	-D	Port Nicholson	8402 BRT	42.11n 69.25w
2132	104	1942-06-16	U-87	CA 3268	XB.25		am	-DP	Cherokee	5896 BRT	.11n 69.25w
3903	192	1945-03-10	U-866	CA 3689	unknown			-D		7000 BRT	
3904	192	1945-03-10	U-866	CA 3689	unknown			-T		7000 BRT	
U-866 heard LUT detonations after 58 sec (premature) and 3:30 min.											

Thomas Weis identified activities of U-boats in the waters off Martha's Vineyard. The majority of activity took place in the first six months of 1942, when Germany was at its strength and the Allied forces had not yet counteracted Nazi dominance at sea.

CHAPTER 27

PRISONER OF WAR
SERGEANT JOSEPH H. SYLVIA

The war hit home for Joseph Sylvia, Oak Bluffs selectman and state representative. Representative Sylvia had worked diligently to orchestrate a deal to create a state beach in Oak Bluffs. In the winter of 1944, a report surfaced that his son, Sergeant Joseph H. Sylvia, was missing in action when he failed to return from a bombing mission over Germany on January 30.

"Sergeant Sylvia is 20 years of age and had been in the Army Air Force for a year on December 1. Serving as a member of the crew of a Flying Fortress, he had made 21 successful missions over enemy territory, and was, presumably, on his 22nd when reported missing."[247]

A month later, details emerged. The B-17, a Flying Fortress, had been hit and was losing altitude. Sergeant Sylvia and his crew parachuted, which lightened the load, allowing the pilot to return safely to England. Sergeant Sylvia was captured.[248] A letter from Sergeant Sylvia reached his parents (written February 28, 1944, received April 28, 1944): "I hope by now you know I am a prisoner of war in Germany. I was wounded, but in good health now."[249]

Sergeant Sylvia was imprisoned in Stalag Luft 4 and later released.[250] His name is on the Oak Bluffs memorial to soldiers who served in World War II. Leonard Vanderhoop, of Gay Head, also was captured and spent time in a POW camp.

CHAPTER 28

D-DAY

As the war turned against the Germans, the Allies continued discussions as to when to launch an invasion of Europe. What was unknown was the exact time and place.

Across Martha's Vineyard, as in communities across the country, D-Day was announced by the ringing of church bells. Henry Beetle Hough wrote about D-Day: "What needed to be said publicly, the church bells said here and there, and not a few Islanders had their first news of the invasion through the sound of the bells. This was D-Day on the Vineyard and weeks from now we shall know what it was like for some of the Island boys who crossed the English Channel by sea or by air to fight for freedom in the world."[251]

On D-Day, before troops landed on the beaches of Normandy, Vineyarders Ted Morgan and Nelson Bryant parachuted into France. Interestingly, the Vineyard ferryboat *New Bedford* was involved as a hospital ship in the initial attack on Omaha Beach on June 6, 1944, and again on Gold Beach on June 10.

Doreen Young was one of three young Red Cross women aboard the *Naushon*, sister ship to the *New Bedford*. "'Yes,' she told the *Gazette* last night, 'I was on the *Naushon* when she was on the Southampton beachhead run after D-Day.' She spoke about getting 'bogged down in the terrific storm which everybody has heard about since, the one which tore so many things to pieces.'"[252]

The hospital ship *Naushon* was not illuminated at D-Day. Machine gun bullets strafed the nursing quarters, but no one was hit. A bomb rocked the ship without injury. The *Naushon* left Normandy on July 4 with 265 casualties and later returned to Utah Beach. *Courtesy of the Mariners' Museum.*

Her story continued:

> *It was a few days after D-Day and we were plying as a hospital ship between Southampton, England and the Omaha beachhead. She was manned by a British crew and had an American medical staff and I was one of three Red Cross girls aboard. Her Captain was a little wiry fellow from the Shetland Islands and a good man.*
>
> *Over and over again the small amphibious craft, carrying a few wounded, would circle round and round us and would then have to return to the beach. It was horrible to see our GIs, bones and flesh broken and torn by jagged shrapnel, pitching on stretchers that were veritable torture racks. The walking wounded were our chief problem. They, poor things, lived down in the hole, accessible only by a perpendicular steel stairway.* [253]

The *Naushon* and *New Bedford* served admirably. "Most of their three war years were spent under the management of Coast Lines running between

Wounded Americans did not relish British rations, so Red Cross women fed the men coffee and doughnuts. Many New England soldiers were aboard the *Naushon* but none from the Vineyard. *Courtesy of the Mariners' Museum.*

Southampton, England and Le Havre, France. During this time the pair ferried over 40,000 Americans across the channel."[254]

"The foreign voyaging of the steamers *Naushon* and *New Bedford* has no precedent," the *Gazette* commented proudly in mid-summer 1944. An editorial crowed, "It makes us, even in this season of transportation trouble, a little glad that they took the side trip across the Atlantic to help in the major matters overseas." A signal corps photograph shows the *Naushon*, "queen of the Island fleet," evacuating wounded from the Normandy fighting front.[255]

Oscar Pease was a well-known Vineyarder. During the war, he was stationed in France but trained in England. He boarded a transport vessel in Le Havre, France, to cross the English Channel, to marry Nellie, his English war bride. As he recounted it, the ship was fog-bound during the crossing. And yet the ship was familiar. He knew where the companionway was; he did not need directions. He was overcome, he said, by an eerie sense of familiarity.

Pease was certain he knew this vessel. Mystified, he wandered onto the outer deck in the fog and saw a life preserver fixed to the bulkhead. He was astonished to see that the name was that of an old Vineyard ferry pressed into wartime service for troop transport on the English Channel.[256]

———·———

"Again, the long arm of coincidence," noted the *Gazette* as the war drew to an end in mid-1945. "Who would have dreamed that a soldier from Martha's Vineyard would have been assigned the task of supervising the repainting of two Island line steamers now in European waters? But that is exactly what happened."[257] Corporal Manuel Burgess of Oak Bluffs had the responsibility of repainting the *Naushon* and *New Bedford* as part of the conversion from hospital ships to transports.

———·———

After the war, the *Naushon* returned to the States and joined the James River Reserve Fleet, where it was converted to an excursion vessel and renamed the *John A. Meseck* and steamed along the Connecticut shoreline. Neither the *New Bedford* nor the *Naushon* ever returned to Vineyard waters. The *Naushon* was sold for scrap in 1974.[258]

CHAPTER 29

END OF THE WAR: 1945

The D-Day invasion marked the beginning of the end of the war, although it took a year to defeat the Nazi forces and fifteen months to bring Japan into submission. Germany signed unconditional surrender with Allied forces on May 7, 1945, just days after Hitler committed suicide. Hostilities in the Pacific theater ended on September 2, 1945, when the foreign affairs minister of Japan surrendered aboard the USS *Missouri* in Tokyo Harbor.

The *Gazette* celebrated:

> *Following the Tuesday night announcement that the Japanese had surrendered, seemingly every down-island Vineyarder, exuberantly for Vineyard behavior, took to the streets with impromptu celebrating. In Oak Bluffs, Edgartown, and Tisbury citizens gathered forming spontaneous parades, cars loaded with passengers, and fire trucks sounding their horns and sirens. Residents lined the streets cheering and crying out, and throwing confetti made on the spot. In Oak Bluffs the streets were so filled with celebrants that without police help, cars could not move on Circuit Avenue.*[259]

"Everyone was so happy when the war was over. All the stores closed, and we'd drive up and down Main Street in a Model T Ford, blowing our horns and [getting] sprayed with water! (We used to call it Main Street instead of Circuit Avenue)." Ruth Metell smiled at her recollection.

Megan Alley shared her joyful memory: "While at a movie one night, hearing band music, we all rushed outside to see what was happening. Up Main Street came Rudy Feibach, the island school instrumental music instructor, leading the band in great celebration as, unbeknownst to us, the war was over. Peace at last."

"Being underage on V-J Day, we were sitting in the Ritz Café on Circuit Avenue celebrating the end of the war." John Boardman remembered the excitement. "Out front, the town hearse drove slowly up the street, pulling a dummy of ToJo [Japan's prime minister] up Circuit Avenue."[260]

Judy Smith remembered fondly: "On the day the war ended, there was a celebratory air in town; people were happy and relieved. My mother took me, my two sisters and brother up to the Rexall Drugstore on Circuit Avenue, and we each had a coffee cabinet." (A cabinet is made up of syrup, milk and ice cream, like a milkshake or frappe.)

Retired Tisbury fire chief Richard Clark recalled, "We had a caravan of teens who drove around and around West Chop to celebrate the war's end." Another Tisbury retired fireman, Bob Tilton, remembered being in a similar parade of cars that drove around East Chop. The end of the war was clearly an all-island event.

"I was on the front porch of Carl Reed's store on V-J Day," recalled Everett Poole. "People were celebrating the end of the war, but I remember feeling somewhat deflated. In just one more year, I would have been eligible to sign up."

Five Nantucket men got together in the Pacific, replicating whaling days when men gammed or visited when they met by chance at sea. "How appropriate that, during a twentieth century world war on a distant Pacific island [Guam], these five Nantucketers would find themselves together for a brief time, sharing a meal and a few thoughts of home."[261]

Joseph McLaughlin, the radioman stationed on Martha's Vineyard, added, "I was often invited to eat dinner by families in town. Home-cooked meals were a great break from the Navy mess. One family had me back two more times because I reminded the Mom of her son who was serving in the south Pacific. I remember well the kindness shown us by the people on the island and I will always remember them."[262]

Megan Alley recalled the war years: "The feelings I had during those times were ones of fear, but also, almost everyone's actions were based on the war effort. We accepted the sounds of the bombings on the south shore, the shortages of gas, shoes and some foodstuffs. It would make our soldiers' lives a little easier and end the war sooner."

Nancy Swift recorded impressions in her diary:

> *Glenn Miller and love songs were so important to us all, which is why the music of the '40s lingers on and brings back tender memories to all of us. We never knew if our loved ones would survive, each moment spent together was tender and precious. Not only with loved ones, but with our dear friends. All of our families shared news, joy and pain with each other and the community embraced us all. I can say when my son was in Vietnam there was no such close and loving support as we had in World War II. Vietnam was a lonely war for families.*

Jane Slater offered a final note:

> *And finally, came the end to the hostilities. It happened in August, when the summer folks were still with us. My mother set out in her Model A Ford to spread the word and soon folks were walking down to the town hall to share the joy with each other. The Model A died in the field and, that may have been its end, however, it had made it through the war years![263]*

CHAPTER 30

POSTWAR

O n June 22, 1945, ninety-two days before World War II officially ended, a Lockheed Lodestar airliner bearing eight passengers landed at the Martha's Vineyard Naval Auxiliary Air Facility.[264] This was the first passenger plane to land at the MVNAAF; it took another year, until October 10, 1946, before the MVNAAF was deeded to Dukes County.

From August 25 to September 8, 1946, the United States Naval Academy football team, complete with instructors, officers, coaches and cadets, was on Martha's Vineyard for a training program that included classes in aviation and academic subjects. Included, of course, was football practice. Captain T.J. Hamilton, USN, a football star on the 1927 champion Academy team, was the group's commander. The officers, coaches, instructors and cadets were housed in the former NAAF barracks. The team practiced at the former gunnery range in Katama with reveille and taps.[265]

The war brought devastation and destruction to many people around the world, yet those on the Vineyard suffered and feared less than most. The three and a half years from December 1941 to May 1945 were desolate and lonely, but Vineyarders worked together.

We are left with munitions, memorials and memories.

More than a quarter century ago, Bob Boren said, "You'll find quite a bit of ordnance out there. You might even find a plane or two out there. I am not surprised by what they found. I know that probably most of it did explode. But there might be one that didn't and that is the danger."[266] Unexploded bombs pose a very real danger to anyone who comes in contact with them. Henry Scott noted, "The munitions, or whatever they could have stored there, could have been covered by the waves and sand. That might account for any burial of munitions there."

Chris Kennedy of the Trustees of Reservations, overseer of South Beach, explains the situation:

> *TCRA stands for Time Critical Removal Action. The TCRA was the first phase of the cleanup effort at Chappy and South Beach to remove any potential explosive ordnance (bombs, rockets and machine gun rounds) from where the public would be likely to come across it. It was believed these warheads were inert, but they took no chances and blew them up on the beach.*

Practice bombs, ammunition and other munitions have washed up over the years. The army conducted two major munitions cleanups, at Cape Poge and Katama, and posted large warnings of potential danger from unexploded munitions. *Photo by Thomas Dresser.*

The U.S. Army Engineering Support Center of Alabama has not found explosive devices in bombs at Katama, according to Ralph Campbell in a telephone interview. "Only a few at Cape Poge and Tisbury Great Pond. Two or three incidents of bombs washed ashore."[267] The TCRA describes munitions finds. Rocket motor body (pipe) was found at Katama, but not explosive. The one-hundred-pound practice bombs at Tisbury and 3.5 bombs at Cape Poge used a black powder charge to ignite; it is an explosive, not enough to kill, yet it could cause injury.

The explosives ordnance disposal team worked at South Beach. "Warheads from rockets were discovered by the underwater recovery crew (divers and surface ordnance personnel)," according to Chris Kennedy. "We still occasionally find live .50-caliber machine gun rounds (brass cartridge, primer and lead bullet) in the sand at Norton Point."

He went on: "The targets for training pilots on the use of 2.25", 3" and 5" rockets were on the beach near left fork and right fork. Army corps has found several thousand rocket motors and warheads along South Beach, including Norton Point, since the two cleanups (early 1990s and again in 2009)."

———·———

Memorials preserve the names of those who served. Even before the war was over, the Edgartown warrant proposed "to see if the town will raise and appropriate the sum of two hundred (200) dollars for construction and maintenance of a War Memorial honor roll for Edgartown men and women in the World War Two service."[268]

Following are Martha's Vineyard town memorials:
Vineyard Haven: 269 servicemen listed at Oak Grove cemetery
Edgartown: 207 names on the plaque by the Dukes County Courthouse
Oak Bluffs: 138 veterans listed on Ocean Park plaque
West Tisbury: 27 servicemen listed by town hall
Chilmark: 26 troops on Beetlebung Corner plaque
Gay Head: 10 servicemen, per Aquinnah town clerk

Our records show 677 people from Martha's Vineyard served in the armed forces during World War II. Two men were prisoners of war, and fourteen servicemen died.[269]

———·———

Above: Twenty-six names are listed on the Chilmark memorial by Beetlebung Corner. The memorial honors "the boys who served God and Country in World War II" and was erected by the Girl Scouts of Chilmark. *Photo by Herb Foster.*

Left: The warrant for the Edgartown town meeting on February 2, 1943, contained an article for a monument for veterans. Other island towns followed suit. *Photo by Thomas Dresser.*

What are we left with? Few vestiges of the war remain beyond town memorials, munitions finds and calcified sandbags on Peaked Hill. The concrete housing at South Beach washed out to sea, as has one of the bunkers at Gay Head. The second bunker serves as an observation post.

We have memories. Vineyarders who were teenagers during the war treasure their recollections. Many Vineyard war veterans have passed on. We value the memories of those who lived through this great conflict. We honor those who died in service and thank those who volunteered on the homefront.

The people of Martha's Vineyard are justly proud that so many efforts were undertaken on-island that contributed to the ultimate victory.

HERB'S STORY

I have a personal interest in the signal corps, having served during World War II. I graduated from high school and turned eighteen on January 31, 1946. I started school at New York University and, after one week of classes, took a leave and enlisted in the United States Army. After basic training at Camp Crowder in Joplin, Missouri, I was assigned to Fort Monmouth in New Jersey to be trained as a 766, high-speed automatic Morse code radio operator. Interestingly, after a few months at Fort Monmouth, someone realized that for many of us, our enlistments would be up before we finished Morse code operator's school. As a result, I was, as the saying goes, shipped out.

Shortly thereafter, I took the train from Penn Station in New York City to Camp Stoneman, the "repple depple" or replacement depot across the bay from San Francisco. After a short stint there, we were marched aboard a ferry in San Francisco Harbor. I will never forget that short march to the ferry. As we walked to the ferry, there was an arch with the saying "Through these portals pass the best damn soldiers in the world." For whatever reason, we walked, carrying our duffel bags, around the arch rather than through it. I still recall saying to myself that someday I'm going to write about this.

We were taken aboard a troop ship and sailed off to the army of occupation of Japan. As I recall, a number of us got what we called at that time Mohawk haircuts as a macho act for going overseas. The moment we went under the San Francisco bridge, it seemed everyone became seasick. For three days, the officers left us alone as far as shaving and other GI details because they were probably sick, too. We were on the *Marine Panther*, one of those Liberty Ships that were prefab and built in a few days at the Kaiser shipyard. The third day is still vivid in my mind, as I began to feel better. We ate standing up against long tables. Suddenly, a GI to my left vomited into his plate, the ship heeled to starboard, his plate slid down in front of me and I threw up into his plate.

About halfway to Japan, a typhoon hit us. We GIs were down below, and the vomit was swishing from side to side as the ship hove back and forth. I couldn't take all the vomit and resulting smell, so I put on my poncho and helmet liner and went up on deck. I opened the door, grabbed the handrail and held on as the ship went down in the ocean troughs and waves came up and over the ship.

As I think about it, that was a foolish thing for me to do. I could have been washed overboard without anyone noticing. I think about what I did and what would have happened when we departed the ship had I been washed overboard. Someone with a clipboard had all our names and serial numbers and stood where the gangplank hit the ground. As you exited, you called off your name and serial number. I could picture him looking around and saying, "Where the hell is this guy?" We were trucked to a repple depple in Yokohama, Japan, to wait assignment.

I was assigned to the Twenty-fourth Infantry Division Signal Company on the Island of Kyushu. Soon after I arrived, we were informed that our regiments were looking for Morse code radio operator volunteers. I volunteered and was assigned to Headquarters Company Thirty-fourth Infantry Regiment of the Twenty-fourth Infantry Division in Sasebo, Japan. I was there six months, sent home and discharged when my enlistment was up.

At one point during my duty, we were hit by a hurricane and had to Jerry rig[270] our equipment so we could be in contact with our three battalions out in Nagasaki. We used our regular radio net equipment as well as what was left of some telephone lines, using both Morse code and voice. Regardless of what we did, we could not communicate. As I recall, the problem was that to use the voice equipment, the button on the handheld equipment had to be held down for sending and receiving. Since none of us had been trained in voice communication, we had no idea what we should have done. With a short period of time left in my enlistment, I took the train to Yokohama, boarded a real troop ship—not a Liberty Ship—and sailed to Seattle and my discharge.

Herb Foster T/5 HQ Co.
Sasebo, Japan

NOTES

Preface

1. George Hough maintained a diary of his experiences on Martha's Vineyard for much of his life. This is an excerpt from 1942.
2. *Vineyard Gazette*, July 7, 1942.
3. Daggett, *It Began with a Whale*, 48.
4. Ibid.

Prologue

5. Herb Foster, *Vineyard Gazette*, January 2, 2014.
6. According to the national census, the population of Martha's Vineyard in 1930 was 4,963; by 1940, it was 5,669.
7. *Martha's Vineyard Magazine*, 1995.

Chapter 1

8. Nazis dressed as Poles staged an attack on a German radio station on August 31, 1939. Hitler used this trumped-up incident to invade Poland.
9. Goodwin, *No Ordinary Time*, 177.
10. Ibid., 233.
11. Ibid., 315.
12. *Vineyard Gazette*, December 6, 1940.

Chapter 2

13. Ibid., October 3, 1941.
14. Bronk, *History of the Eastern Defense Command*, 7.
15. Ibid., 33.
16. Ibid, 63.
17. Bishop, *Prints in the Sand*, 22.
18. Ibid., 24.

19. *Vineyard Gazette,* July 22, 1988.
20. Bishop, *Prints in the Sand.*
21. Dogs for Defense was a program to use dogs in defending the homeland. Selected dogs were used in patrols by coastguardsmen around Martha's Vineyard. German shepherds proved the most effective. Henry Beetle Hough's dog, a collie named Matrix, was a fixture at the *Vineyard Gazette* and was written about to seek donations for the War Dog Fund.
22. Allen, "Nantucket Goes to War," 15.
23. Bronk, *History of the Eastern Defense Command*, Narragansett Bay, 7.
24. Witzell, "Life in Woods Hole," 28.
25. Ibid., 13.
26. Cimino, *Camp Edwards*, 7.

Chapter 3

27. *Dukes County Intelligencer*, May 1987, 186.
28. Letter from President Roosevelt to Margaret Suckley, USS *Augusta*, August 23, 1941.
29. In *Masters and Commanders*, 52, Andrew Roberts wrote, "In a nine-page handwritten letter on 4 August to his cousin and confidante Margaret 'Daisy' Suckley, Roosevelt described how he had been secretly transferred from his presidential yacht the *Potomac* on to the heavy cruiser USS *Augusta*, and with another cruiser and five destroyers as escort, had made his way to Newfoundland." According to the notes, a Conrad Black, who lives in Toronto, has the original letter.
30. *Vineyard Gazette*, August 5, 1941.
31. Ibid.
32. Cray, *General of the Army*, 210.
33. *Dukes County Intelligencer*, 187.
34. Roosevelt, letter from FDR to Margaret Suckley, August 20, 1941.
35. Hough, *Once More the Thunderer*, 195.
36. *Dukes County Intelligencer*, 1987, 187.

Chapter 4

37. *Martha's Vineyard Magazine*, September–October 2004.
38. Railton, *History of Martha's Vineyard*, 387.
39. *Martha's Vineyard Magazine*, 2004.
40. Railton, *History of Martha's Vineyard*, 397.

Chapter 5

41. Francis Fisher served in the Third Division, with a rank of technical sergeant. As a teenager, he caddied at the Edgartown Golf Club.

42. Local 173 is now Post 257.
43. *Vineyard Gazette,* July 4, 1941.
44. Ibid., October 17, 1941.
45. Ibid.
46. Ibid.

Chapter 6

47. After the war, Nancy Hazelton Swift Franke moved off-island to Medfield, Massachusetts. Her father was Dean Ripley Swift. Nancy had six children and seven grandchildren.
48. *Vineyard Gazette,* December 12, 1941.
49. Ibid., March 19, 1943.

Chapter 7

50. Bishop, *Prints in the Sand,* 22.
51. Dagnall, *Martha's Vineyard Camp Meeting Association,* 84–86.
52. Schofield, *In the Beginning…Alpha.*
53. *Vineyard Gazette,* December 19, 1941.
54. Ibid., January 16, 1942.
55. Lee, *Those Who Serve,* 53.
56. *Vineyard Gazette,* July 10, 1942.
57. Ibid., August 25, 1942.
58. *Annual Report of the Town of Oak Bluffs,* 1943, 88.
59. *Annual Report of the Town of Edgartown,* 1943, 114.
60. *Annual Report of the Town of Oak Bluffs,* 1943, 80.
61. *Vineyard Gazette,* December 12, 1941.
62. Freeman Leonard's mother successfully urged that the steamships be painted white after the war.
63. Bishop, *Prints in the Sand,* 22.

Chapter 8

64. *Vineyard Gazette,* June 18, 1943.
65. Ibid., October 8, 1943.
66. Lee, *Those Who Serve,* 137–39.

Chapter 9

67. Schneider, *Enduring Shore,* 140.
68. *Annual Report of the Chief Signal Officer,* 153.
69. Ibid., 154.
70. *Report of the Adjutant-General,* 119–20, 123–24.
71. Rescue 21 replaced the National Distress and Response System used since the 1970s. According to the coast guard, "Rescue 21 is the Coast Guard's advanced

command, control and direction-finding communications system to better locate mariners in distress and save lives and property at sea and on navigable rivers." www.uscg.mil/acquistion/rescue21.

72. VOLF press release, November 2, 1999.
73. *Martha's Vineyard Land Bank Commission*, 37–39, 57.
74. *Nantucket Magazine*, 1994.

Chapter 10

75. *Vineyard Gazette*, January 2, 1942.
76. Schofield, *In the Beginning…Alpha*.
77. *Vineyard Gazette*, May 8, 1942.
78. Lee, *More Vineyard Voices*, 302.
79. *Nantucket Magazine*, 1994.
80. Ibid.; *Vineyard Gazette*, 1923 (actually May 26, 1944; wrong year in the masthead).
81. Lee, *More Vineyard Voices*, 302.
82. Lee, *Those Who Serve*, 153.

Chapter 11

83. *Annual Report of the Town of Oak Bluffs*, 1940, 116.

Chapter 12

84. Lee, *More Vineyard Voices*, 136–37.
85. Farson, *Cape Cod Railroads*, 249.
86. Ibid.

Chapter 13

87. *Vineyard Gazette*, November 14, 1941.
88. Ibid., December 12, 1941.
89. Ibid., January 16, 1942.
90. Ibid., January 23, 1942.
91. Ibid., July 3, 1942.
92. Ibid.
93. Ibid., September 4, 1942.
94. Ibid., May 21, 1943.
95. Ibid., July 16, 1943.
96. Ibid., October 29, 1943.

Chapter 14

97. Lee, *More Vineyard Voices*, 59.
98. Ibid., 58.

99. Ibid., 59.
100. Goodwin, *No Ordinary Time*, 523.
101. Ibid.
102. Executive Order No. 9981 was issued by President Truman on July 26, 1948. The order stated, "It is hereby declared to be the policy of the President that there shall be equality of treatment and opportunity for all persons in the armed services without regard to race, color, religion, or national origin."
103. Lee, *Those Who Serve*, 61–62.

Chapter 15

104. Lee, *Vineyard Voices*, 139.
105. Witzell, "Life in Woods Hole," 31.
106. Ibid.
107. Lee, *Those Who Serve*, 62.
108. *Vineyard Gazette*, October 29, 1943.
109. Ibid.
110. Ibid., letter from Cyril Norton, December 3, 1943.
111. Ibid., August 15, 1944.
112. Ibid., January 26, 1945.
113. Ibid., July 13, 1945.

Chapter 16

114. Ibid., January 9, 1942.
115. Ibid., May 29, 1942.
116. Ibid., July 10, 1942.
117. A poster for the event is on display at the Art Cliff Diner in Vineyard Haven.
118. *Vineyard Gazette*, July 31, 1942.
119. Lee, *More Vineyard Voices*, 39.
120. *Vineyard Gazette*, August 18, 1944.

Chapter 17

121. Schofield, *In the Beginning…Alpha*.
122. Ibid.
123. *Vineyard Gazette*, July 24, 1942.
124. Ibid., July 28, 1942.
125. Schofield, *In the Beginning…Alpha*.

Chapter 18

126. *Vineyard Gazette*, May 6, 1949.
127. Ibid., July 10, 1942.
128. Ibid., August 7, 1942.

129. *Stars & Stripes.*
130. Shaum, "Honeymoon Fleet," 67.
131. Ibid.
132. *Vineyard Gazette,* June 6, 1995.
133. Shaum, "Honeymoon Fleet," 67.
134. *Vineyard Gazette,* May 6, 1949.
135. Witzell, "Life in Woods Hole," 28.
136. *Stars & Stripes,* August 25, 1943.

Chapter 19

137. *Vineyard Gazette,* May 22, 1942.
138. William Colby owned the Martha's Vineyard Shipyard with his partner, William Dugan. Colby also owned the asphalt pit at Goodale's that provided tar for the roadways leading to the airfield. Colby had two sons; one died in the war, and the other died at the asphalt plant.
139. This quote was on the back of the photo of the boat made at Colby's.
140. *Vineyard Gazette,* January 15, 1943.
141. Ibid.
142. Ibid., March 19, 1943.
143. Ibid., June 18, 1943.
144. Ibid., May 5, 1944.

Chapter 20

145. Ibid., July 7, 1942.
146. Becker, *Amphibious Training Center.*
147. Ibid.
148. Ibid.
149. Ibid.
150. Ibid.
151. Cimino, *Camp Edwards,* 12.
152 Daggett, *It Began with a Whale,* 48.
153. Phelan, *From Carrier Pigeons to Carrier Pilots,* 5.
154. Galluzzo, *Camp Edwards,* 104–5.
155. *Vineyard Gazette,* October 9, 1942.
156. Cimino, *Camp Edwards,* 13.
157. Galluzzo, *Camp Edwards,* 103–4.
158. Cimino, *Through Soldiers' Eyes.*
159. *Falmouth Enterprise,* October 9, 1942.
160. *Vineyard Gazette,* October 9, 1942.
161. Ibid.
162. Phelan, *From Carrier Pigeons to Carrier Pilots,* 6.
163. *Vineyard Gazette,* October 9, 1942.
164. Ibid.

165. Becker, *Amphibious Training Center*.
166. In the spring of 1943, the Engineer Amphibian Brigade traveled to Carrabelle, Florida, for further training. The brigade, made up of 303 officers, returned to the Cape in mid-June, traveling 2,170 miles in thirty-eight landing craft and small boats.
167. *Vineyard Gazette*, July 22, 1988.
168. Hough, *Once More the Thunderer*, 213.
169. Cimino, *Camp Edwards*, 13.
170. *Vineyard Gazette*, May 14, 1943.
171. Ibid., May 26, 1944.
172. Ibid.,
173. Scott, "Navy Combat Pilots," November 1981, 79.
174. Ibid.
175. *Vineyard Gazette*, March 31, 1944.
176. Ibid.
177. Ibid.
178. *Falmouth Enterprise*, reprinted in the *Vineyard Gazette*, January 21, 1944.

Chapter 21

179. *Vineyard Gazette*, January 1, 1943.
180. Ibid., August 3, 1943.
181. Ibid.
182. Ibid., December 10, 1943.
183. Quonset huts were portable structures first manufactured at Quonset Point, Rhode Island. They were prefabricated pieces of corrugated, galvanized steel, easier to transport than tents. The basic size was sixteen feet by thirty-six feet.
184. *Dukes County Intelligencer*, 1984, 126.
185. Ibid.
186. Carol Charette, New England District of Army Corps of Engineers, Concord, MA, e-mail January 15, 2014.

Chapter 22

187. Look, Luce and Norton, "Report of the County Commissioners," 69–70.
188. Lee, *More Vineyard Voices*, 50.
189. Waller, "Impact of Civil Defense."
190. *Vineyard Gazette*, March 26, 1943.
191. Ibid., April 16, 1943.
192. Lee, *More Vineyard Voices*, 144.
193. Ibid.
194. Ibid., 145.
195. Ibid.
196. *Martha's Vineyard Magazine*, 1995.

197. *Vineyard Gazette*, May 4, 1945.
198. Ibid.
199. Lee, *Those Who Serve*, 155.
200. Lee, *More Vineyard Voices*, 51.
201. *Vineyard Gazette*, January 21, 1944.
202. Lee, *More Vineyard Voices*, 146.

Chapter 23

203. Ibid., 51.
204. *Martha's Vineyard Magazine*, Dunlop, 1995.
205. *Vineyard Gazette*, December 5, 1958.
206. Ibid., July 29, 1958.
207. Ibid., August 31, 1943.
208. Ibid., October 22, 1943.
209. Ibid., December 24, 1943.
210. Ibid., June 2, 1944.
211. Ibid., August 18, 1944.
212. Ibid., September 9, 1944.
213. Ibid., February 16, 1945.
214. Ibid., July 3, 1942.
215. Ibid.
216. Skiffs Island no longer exists. It was off Wasque Shoal, halfway between Martha's Vineyard and Nantucket, in the Muskegat Channel. Hauser Island is nearby.
217. *Vineyard Gazette*, July 2, 1943.

Chapter 24

218. Ibid., August 31, 1945.
219. Ibid.
220. Ibid.
221. Ibid., September 17, 1943.
222. Ibid.
223. Ibid.
224. Ibid.
225. Ibid.
226. Hough, *Once More the Thunderer*, 217.
227. Galland, *The First and the Last*, 217.
228. Waller, "Impact of Civil Defense," 5.

Chapter 25

229. Morgan, Captain, USN, letter, July 3, 1943.
230. *Vineyard Gazette*, February 4, 1944.

231. Ibid.
232. Ibid., July 22, 1988.
233. Ibid.
234. Ibid.
235. Ibid.

Chapter 26

236. *Boston Globe*, November 3, 2013.
237. Ibid.
238. Lee, *Those Who Serve*, 137–39.
239. Lee, *More Vineyard Voices*, 137.
240. Lee, *Vineyard Voices*, 22.
241. Lee, *Those Who Serve*, 157.
242. Connole, *26ᵗʰ "Yankee" Division*, 118.
243. Ibid.
244. Ibid., 126.
245. Ibid.
246. Details of the landings may be obtained from the Department of the Navy, Naval Historical Center, Washington, D.C. German Espionage and Sabotage Against the U.S. in World War II; National Archives and Records Administration, College Park, MD 20740.

Chapter 27

247. *Vineyard Gazette*, February 18, 1944.
248. Ibid., March 3, 1944.
249. Ibid., May 5, 1944.
250. Information on Sergeant Sylvia can be found at aad.archives.gov/aad/display-partial-records.jsp?f=645&mtch=8&q=sylvia&cat=all&dt=466&tf=F&bc=sl,sd. (Interestingly, this is the same POW camp where Bradford Truesdell, of Jefferson, Massachusetts, a neighbor of Thomas Dresser, was imprisoned. Truesdell also parachuted from a B-17, was captured and imprisoned in the Stalag Luft 4. www.stalagluft4.org/pdf/janis%20roster.pdf.)

Chapter 28

251. Hough, *Once More the Thunderer*, 234.
252. *Vineyard Gazette*, June 13, 1995. Interview with Doreen Young, of Carlisle, Massachusetts, 1946.
253. Ibid., June 13, 1995.
254. Steamboat Bill, "*Naushon* and *New Bedford* at War," 201–2.
255. *Vineyard Gazette*, August 4, 1944.

256. Interview with Grace Sullivan, January 23, 2014.
257. *Vineyard Gazette*, July 3, 1945.
258. Shaum, "Honeymoon Fleet."

Chapter 29

259. *Vineyard Gazette*, August 17, 1945.
260. Hideki Tojo was prime minister of Japan and was executed as a war criminal.
261. *Historic Nantucket*, 1993.
262. Letter received October 21, 2013, from Joseph McLaughlin.
263. Lee, *Those Who Serve*, 139.

Chapter 30

264. *Martha's Vineyard Magazine*, 1995.
265. *Vineyard Gazette*, August 23, 1946.
266. Ibid., July 22, 1988.
267. Ralph Campbell, project manager, Ordnance and Explosives Design Center, U.S. Army Engineering Support Center, Huntsville, Alabama. Phone call, January 14, 2014.
268. *Annual Report of the Town of Edgartown*, 1943, 106.
269. We encountered disparity in the number of veterans. Town memorials list 677 veterans, counted by Geo Meikle, Tom's "Little Brother." In his *History of Martha's Vineyard*, Arthur Railton counts 614 by soldiers from each branch of the service. And the *Vineyard Gazette* of May 4, 1945, lists 585 veterans.

Afterword

270. The term "Jerry rig" originated during World War II. Germans were called Jerries. Allies came across hastily repaired objects they left behind, hence the term Jerry rig.

BIBLIOGRAPHY

Becker, Captain Marshall O. *The Amphibious Training Center, Study No. 22.* N.p.: self-published, 1946.

Bishop, Eleanor. *Prints in the Sand: The U.S. Coast Guard Beach Patrols in World War II.* Missoula, MT: Pictorial Histories Publishing Co., 1989.

Bronk, William. *A History of the Eastern Defense Command.* N.p.: self-published, 1945. Courtesy of Mark Berhow.

Cimino, Anthony. *Camp Edwards in World War II.* N.p.: self-published, 1993.

Connole, Dennis. *The 26ᵗʰ "Yankee" Division on Coast Patrol Duty, 1942–1943.* Jefferson, NC: McFarland & Co., 2008.

Cray, Ed. *General of the Army.* New York: W.W. Norton & Company, 1990.

Daggett, John Tobey. *It Began with a Whale.* Somerville, MA: Fleming and Son, 1963.

Dagnall, Sally. *Martha's Vineyard Camp Meeting Association 1835–1985.* Oak Bluffs, MA: MV Camp Meeting Association, 1984.

Farson, Robert. *Cape Cod Railroads.* Yarmouth, MA: Cape Cod Historical Publications, 1977.

Galland, Adolf. *The First and the Last: The Rise and Fall of the German Fighter Forces, 1938–1945.* Cutchogue, NY: Buccaneer Books, 1954.

Galluzzo, John. *Camp Edwards and Otis Air Force Base.* Mount Pleasant, SC: Arcadia, 2010.

Goodwin, Doris Kearns. *No Ordinary Time.* New York: Simon & Schuster, 1994.

Hough, Henry Beetle. *Once More the Thunderer.* New York: Ives Washburn, Inc., 1950.

Lee, Linsey. *More Vineyard Voices.* Edgartown, MA: Martha's Vineyard Historical Society, 2005.

———. *Those Who Serve: Martha's Vineyard and World War II.* Edgartown, MA: Martha's Vineyard Museum, 2011.

———. *Vineyard Voices.* Edgartown, MA: Martha's Vineyard Historical Society, 1998.

Look, Hosea S., Stephen C. Luce Jr. and Frank L. Norton. "Report of the County Commissioners." *Annual Reports of the Town Officers of the Town of Edgartown for the Year Ending December 31, 1943.* Oak Bluffs, MA: Martha's Vineyard Printing Co., 1943.

Morison, Samuel Eliot. *The Battle of the Atlantic: September 1939–May 1943.* Boston: Little, Brown and Company, 1970.

Phelan, Dr. Robert. *From Carrier Pigeons to Carrier Pilots: Overview of World War II Military Action on Cape Cod and the Islands.* N.p.: self-published, n.d.

Railton, Arthur. *The History of Martha's Vineyard*. Beverly, MA: Commonwealth Editions and Martha's Vineyard Historical Society, 2006.

Roberts, Andrew. *Masters and Commanders: How Four Titans Won the War in the West, 1941–1945*. New York: Harper and Row, 2009.

Taylor, Theodore. *Fire on the Beaches*. New York: W.W. Norton & Company, 1958.

Schneider, Paul. *The Enduring Shore: A History of Cape Cod, Martha's Vineyard and Nantucket*. New York: Henry Holt, 2000.

Schofield, Jay. *In the Beginning...Alpha*. N.p.: self-published, 2007.

Waller, Christian. "The Impact of Civil Defense and Military Measures Implemented on Martha's Vineyard During World War II." Thesis, 1993.

Werner, Herbert A. *Iron Coffins: A Personal Account of the German U-Boat Battles of World War II*. New York: Holt, Rinehart and Winston, 1969.

Reports and Periodicals

Allen, Jean. "Nantucket Goes to War." *Historic Nantucket* 41, no. 6 (Spring 1993).

Annual Report of the Chief Signal Officer for the Army to the Secretary for War. Washington, D.C.: Government Printing Office, 1887.

Annual Report of the Town of Edgartown. Oak Bluffs, MA: Martha's Vineyard Printing Co., 1943.

Annual Report of the Town of Oak Bluffs. Oak Bluffs, MA: Martha's Vineyard Printing Co., 1940, 1941, 1942, 1943, 1944.

Boston Globe

Cimino, LTC Anthony. *Through Soldiers' Eyes* (video). Falmouth Library.

Dresser, Thomas. "Independence Days." *Vineyard Style*, Summer 2008.

Falmouth Enterprise

Martha's Vineyard Land Bank Commission, Peaked Hill Management Plan. Martha's Vineyard, MA: Land Bank, 1993.

Martha's Vineyard Magazine, 1995, 2004.

Mooney, Robert F. "On the Nantucket Home Front." *Nantucket Magazine*, Summer 1994.

Report of the Adjutant-General State of Connecticut to the Commander in Chief, Captain William F.M. Rogers, Commanding Brigade Signal Corps. C.N.G. Bridgeport, CT: Marigold Printing, 1889.

Scott, Henry. "Navy Combat Pilots Train at Island Air Base." *Dukes County Intelligencer*, February 1984.

Shaum, Jack. "The Honeymoon Fleet." *Sea Classics*, 2004.

Stars & Stripes, August 25, 1943.

Steamboat Bill. "Naushon & New Bedford at War." Steamship Historical Society of America, Inc. #128, Winter 1973.

Vineyard Gazette

Wilderstein Historic Site, Rhinebeck, New York. Duane Watson, Curator. Letter from FDR to Margaret Suckley, August 20, 1941.

Witzell, Susan Fletcher. "Life in Woods Hole Village during World War II." *Spiritsail*, Woods Hole Museum, Winter 1995.

INDEX

The authors in the field, *left to right*: Thomas Dresser, Herb Foster and Jay Schofield. Bud Mayhew led a tour of Peaked Hill, where he pointed out a tree that had grown through a chain-link fence and sandbags calcified by time. *Photo by Bud Mayhew.*

ABOUT THE AUTHORS

Herb Foster, of Edgartown, was a World War II veteran. He was a New York City teacher and administrator and is professor emeritus at SUNY-Buffalo. Herb's father, Max, served with the AEF in France; Herb's brother Jerry was wounded fighting with the Eighty-fifth ID in Italy in World War II, and his brother Jack served in the Korean War. Herb has written many articles, as well as the book *Ribbin', Jivin', and Playin' the Dozens: The Persistent Dilemma in Our Schools*. Herb is completing *Ghetto to Ghetto: Yiddish and Jive in Everyday Life*. He is also a trustee of the Edgartown Library.

Jay Schofield, of Vineyard Haven and son of a World War II veteran, has written numerous personal memoirs and books on American history, as well as a book on basketball coaching and one on metal detecting. He is an island tour guide. Visit jayschofield.com for more information.

Tom Dresser, of Oak Bluffs, is a baby-boomer, born after the war was over. His father, Waldo Lincoln Dresser, served in the coast guard from Block Island to Normandy to the Pacific. Tom drives a school bus and has written books for The History Press and booklets on local communities. For more information, visit tomdresser.com.